Disclaimer

This book is designed for educational purposes only. The services of a competent professional trainer or applied behaviorist should be sought regarding its applicability with respect to your own dog. The training of dogs is not without risk. The author and publisher shall have neither liability nor responsibility to any person or entity with respect to any loss or damage caused or alleged to be caused directly or indirectly by the information contained in this book.

If you do not wish to be bound by the above, you may return this book to the publisher for a full refund.

© 2002 Jean Donaldson
All rights reserved
Printed in the United States of America

Requests for permission to reprint should be sent to:

The Academy for Dog Trainers
info@academyfordogtrainers.com

D0376582

ISBN 978-0-9705629-4-4

A Guide to Resource Guarding in Dogs

Contents

I.   Introduction

IV.   Adjuncts, Regressions and Prevention

A Guide to Resource Guarding in Dogs

Introduction

This manual is about dogs who growl, snarl, snap and bite when you try to take things away from them, approach them when they are eating or when they have claimed some other resource, such as their owner or a comfy sleeping location. This is a remarkably common problem but, luckily, can often be successfully resolved and even prevented.

Acknowledging the Bar

There continues to be rampant animosity towards dogs with aggression problems. My Academy co-instructor, Janis, has pointed out that the attitude, at least here in the US, used to be more relaxed. In a hilarious James Thurber story, a woman sends boxes of chocolates at Christmas to everyone the dog bit that year. One year she sent out 50 boxes. A crotchety dog was more taken in stride and cause for humorous annoyance than cause for litigation, as it would be today. Dogs were animals and animals sometimes bit.

1

There's no doubt that a generally more litigious society is part of the picture today. But dogs seem a particularly emotional issue. Comparable injuries caused by, say, opening a can in the kitchen and being bitten by a dog are rarely treated the same way. The latter is more likely to be presented in an emergency room. Every time there is a dog-related fatality, there is pressure on lawmakers to ban breeds of dogs, muzzle all dogs or somehow better protect the public. Yet, the public is at far greater lethal risk from lawnmowers. One is far more likely to be struck by lightning several times or be killed by a power shovel than to ever be killed by a dog. Infant fatalities are a great deal more likely to be associated with 25-gallon plastic barrels than with dog attacks, yet no one is calling for a ban on these. Kids are also astronomically more likely to be injured or killed by a parent or guardian. Our expectations of dogs are high.

Our expectations of dogs are *very* high, actually. The standard we have set for them is one we would consider absurd for any other species of animal, including ourselves. We want no aggressive behavior directed at humans, of even the most ritualized sort, at any time, over the entire course of the dog's life. This is exactly like you going a lifetime without ever once losing your temper, swearing at another driver in traffic, being rude to someone in a line-up, writing a hot letter to the editor, defending yourself from what you perceive to be a threat, calling a lawyer or saying something mean to your spouse that you later regret. All species-normal, even highly ritualized aggression forbidden.

As if this weren't enough, we also want dogs to suddenly be **very** aggressive if a crime is being perpetrated against us. We want the dog to be able to tell the good guys from the bad guys and guard our own coveted resources! We even breed dogs with this in mind, flirting with the deliberate selection of traits such as "wary of strangers," "one man" or "one family dog" or other euphemisms that suggest we don't want dogs to be entirely gregarious and easy to socialize. It doesn't occur to us the extreme unlikelihood of achieving through selective breeding a dog who is more likely to guard a stereo than a meaty bone.

I am not suggesting we don't take dog aggression seriously and do everything we can to eliminate it. What I am suggesting is that a good start for this effort would be acknowledging the bar we are setting. It is extremely predictable that dogs, like all animals, will behave aggressively when they are afraid or feel threatened and in order to defend resources. If we would like to have this never, or almost never, happen, we will have to insert multiple lines of defense, starting with facing up to the biological legacy we are up against.

Ritualization: Levels of Protracted Threat

When I get angry or feel wronged, there is a big difference between suing you or being rude to you and pulling out a firearm and shooting at you. Although all are aggressive acts, one kind is ritualized and one is not. Our laws reflect our recognition that some kinds of conflict resolution and aggression are okay and some are not. The essence of this difference is the degree of damage inflicted. Sports – which are inherently about winning in a conflict situation - make this distinction as well. The ubiquity of rules in sport implies that we agree on a need for rules and conventions governing how we can engage in them.

Similarly, there is a big difference in ritualized and non-ritualized conflict resolution behavior in dogs. Hard stares, growling, snarling, snapping and biting without maiming force are the "legal" conflict resolution behaviors in dog society. They are ways for dogs to settle conflicts – to say "back off!" if you will - without the high price to all participants of flat-out uninhibited aggression. Dogs are equipped with maim-force

3

jaws, capable of crushing bone and tearing flesh. They carry these heavy weapons with them at all times, yet have managed to not self-annihilate as a species, in spite of lots of arguing about bones, mates and carcasses. The reason is a long history of selection for well-developed ritualization.

The following are components of ritualized aggression in dogs. They communicate the internal state and willingness to guard to the approaching threat, and advertise agonistic capability ("See these teeth? Hear this big growl? I'd be a formidable opponent in a fight..."). Accelerated consumption is specific to warning competitors away from resources; the rest are used in all types of "back off" situations.

1) Freezing up

Also called "hard-eyeing," a glassy-eyed stare accompanies a cessation of activity. If the dog was chewing, he stops chewing. If the dog was eating, he stops eating. The stare is oblique, rarely directly at the approaching threat. Owners may report the hard, detached, spaced out looking expression, mistaking it for some sort of seizure.

2) Accelerated consumption

In contrast to a cessation of consumption, acceleration is just that: if the dog was eating, he starts eating faster, almost punching at the food. If the dog was chewing, he starts chewing faster and more intensely.

3) Growl

The low, steady and ominous rumbling that dogs are capable of emanating can be on its own or simultaneous with other threats.

4) Snarl

Exposing the teeth by vertically retracting the lips may also occur before, after or simultaneous to other threat signals. Each dog's style of delivering protracted warning may differ.

5) Snap

A snap is an air-bite - dog deliberately misses. People frequently report that a dog tried to bite them but missed or else they were able to move away quickly enough. This is unlikely, as a geriatric, couch-potato dog has a reaction time better than an Olympic athlete. When dogs intend to bite, they bite. When they intend to snap, they snap.

6) Inhibited bite

When a dog bites and no damage is done, the dog is said to have good acquired bite inhibition or a "soft" or "good" mouth. It has been speculated that this capability of biting without damage is acquired prior to 4 months of age through the mechanism of free-play with other puppies. In fact, puppies are thought to have such sharp, needle-like teeth is *so that it will* hurt when they bite other puppies. Puppies need feedback in the form of play interruptions for overly hard biting, but their jaws are too weak to cause pain with pressure alone. Hence the sharp teeth. For detailed information on installing soft mouth in puppies, read Ian Dunbar's *How to Teach a New Dog Old Tricks* or his other superb books on puppy training.

Dogs with soft mouths have rosier prognoses than dogs who inflict damaging bites. They can be treated more aggressively as the risk is so much lower should the dog offend during or between training sessions. Owners are understandably reluctant to work on a dog who has seriously injured a family member.

The Adaptive Significance of Resource Guarding

I'm continually impressed by the degree to which behaviors that are no longer under any evolutionary selective pressure show up in pet dogs. Resource guarding – dogs behaving aggressively when in possession of (and sometimes to gain possession of) food, toys, bones, their owners, their resting spots and crates – is a prime example. After scores of generations of dog breeders selecting for conformation and various work functions and steady provision of food and other resources that would render obsolete the relatively expensive behavior of guarding them, a significant proportion of pet dogs guard things, from other dogs and from people, including their guardians who have done all the providing! If anything, there is selection pressure against this trait, as our society has a very low tolerance of aggression towards people, especially family members, the context where resource guarding is most often presented. Guarders might be more likely to be euthanized. Yet the trait is alive and well in the population at large.

It is easy to see how, in a natural environment, a group-hunting carnivore who guards would have reproductive advantage over one who gladly relinquishes. It's a good trait, like a well-developed immune system or legs that can run fast. In a domestic environment, it is undesired.

Fallacies About Resource Guarding

1) That it is abnormal behavior.

Guarding food, coveted objects, mates and physical space, as we've seen, are highly adaptive traits in a natural environment. If dogs had to fend for themselves tomorrow, guarders would have the survival and reproductive edge over non-guarders.

6

2) That because it is largely genetically driven, rather than learned, it is immutable.

This fallacy is not limited to resource guarding. While it is true that genetic programming can make certain behaviors easier to learn in some cases or interfere with learning in other cases, there is no neat correlation between how much a behavior is thought to be genetically influenced and its susceptibility to behavior modification.

The environment selects behavior in two parallel ways. One by conferring advantage to individuals in possession of DNA that potentiates certain behavior and one by conferring advantage to individuals who readily learn a behavior during their lifetime. The nature/nurture question is a false dichotomy. When you find yourself asking whether a behavior is "learned" or "genetic," the answer is always: both.

3) That it can be cured by making the dog realize that resources are abundant.

This logic-based approach tries to convince the dog that there's no reason to guard, as resources are plentiful. Alas, it would seem dogs do not learn this way though, luckily, they do respond to other measures described later.

4) That it is a symptom of a dominant or pushy personality in a dog.

This is largely a legacy of the pervasiveness of social hierarchy models as explanation for so much of dog behavior as well as springboards for treatment techniques. A massive percentage of dog owners have a sketchy, if any, understanding of how to apply even the most basics techniques of operant and classical conditioning, yet virtually all owners can throw around the word "dominance" with abandon. The explanation of resource guarding as being all about rank also fits nicely with the medical model of symptom-diagnosis as well as having provided decades of justification for the use of aversives in training.

However, resource guarding responds well to desensitization and counterconditioning and to well-executed operant techniques, which raises questions about dominance. When the dog stops guarding his food and toys, has he become less dominant as a result of the desensitization and counterconditioning? If so, by what mechanism? Is rank therefore not a fixed trait? If not, can one still say a dog is a "dominant" dog? If dominance is a relationship rather than a trait, how could simple desensitization/counterconditioning exercises change the relationship? Part of the elegance of the behaviorist paradigm is that it provides a much simpler way to describe post-treatment behavior.

It also bears mentioning that a large percentage of resource guarders present with other problems, like submissive urination, shyness or lack of confidence, that would seem diametrically opposed to the concept that the dog is overly assertive (i.e. "dominant"). Once again, carefully documenting what the dog is doing and then employing operant and classical conditioning to change that is both more parsimonious and efficacious.

People may also think that a dog who is inclined to guard resources is not a "nice" dog. I guess this depends on how you define "nice." Many of the nicest dogs I know, including my own two Border Collies, are rampant resource guarders, reformed with conditioning. They were and are "nice" dogs in the opinions of virtually everyone who has met them.

    5)   That it is a result of "spoiling" the dog.

Resource guarding is an equal opportunity behavior problem. It crops up in young and old, in all breeds and dogs with all kinds of life histories. "Spoiled" is also a very subjective term. I am dismayed at how people label dogs spoiled when their basic needs are being met, when they are simply well loved and their lives are relatively free of aversives. Dogs are often also so labeled when their owners are struggling with getting the operant contingencies under their control: when dogs are barking to get what they want, being rude, unruly and disobedient etc. There is no evidence, however, that poor obedience has anything to do with resource guarding. Many dogs with stellar obedience and manners present with resource guarding, and many dogs with both problems can have their resource guarding resolved without touching their crummy obedience, though it is of course possible to address both.

Kinds of Resource Guarding

Dogs may guard food and/or food bowl, coveted toys or objects, their owners, or choice sleeping locations. Dogs often present with more than one kind of guarding and may also have body-handling problems. Of course, resource guarders may happen to also have any of a number of other behavior problems, but the most common constellation will involve guarding more than one kind of resource and being uncomfortable about certain kinds of body handling.

Although it may be tempting to point to the trend towards different forms of resource guarding co-occurring as evidence of an underlying syndrome or condition (such as dominance), in the behaviorist model, there is no need to invoke additional constructs aside from the observable behavior in order to explain or modify it.

Food Guarding

This is the most common kind of resource guarding and can look like one or more of the following:

- The dog threatens or bites when approached while eating from his bowl
- The dog threatens or bites when the owner tries to retrieve a food item the dog has snatched
- The dog threatens or bites when approached after he comes upon some sort of food item in the gutter

The presence and severity of food guarding is usually entirely dependent on the value or palatability of the food in question. If a dog is not motivated by a particular food item, this in no way rules him out as a guarder if he does not guard that item. The only true rule-out of food guarding is removal of food the dog is highly motivated to consume. Some dogs may be compulsive, guarding all food items and even an empty dish in a very reflexive looking fashion, but the majority will guard only when actually in possession of sufficiently motivating food.

Object Guarding

Object guarding can crop up in any dog. The severity of guarding, once again, is largely dependent on the value of the item to the dog. Commonly guarded objects include: bones, rawhides and pigs' ears (these ambiguous items could be also be classified as food), favorite toys and balls, laundry items, Kleenexes, wrappers and other garbage, and sticks and "forbidden fruit" objects, i.e. items the dog steals whose value is augmented by its novelty, extreme owner reaction and/or its inherent features.

Location Guarding

The most common location guarding scenarios are:

- A dog who won't let the owner or a spouse into the bed or bedroom once the dog is lying on the bed
- A dog who is grumpy and aggressive when jostled on

10

❑ A dog who threatens passersby and/or dogs when he is in his crate or in the car

An interesting feature of all resource guarding is that its severity may not only be tied to the value of the resource, but also to who is approaching. Location guarding, such as a dog who seems to let the wife but not the husband in the bed, is a prime example.

Owner Guarding

Dogs may be selectively aggressive when approached – most notably approach by other dogs, though people can also be targets – if they are in proximity of their owners or when on leash. Some owners find the "jealous" behavior  flattering or amusing, while others are distressed. Owners often attribute the behavior to "protectiveness." The topography of the behavior is identical to other kinds of resource guarding, and it responds to the same kinds of treatment exercises, so it would seem logical to consider the owner a coveted resource in these cases.

Miscellaneous Guarding

Dogs may also guard other dogs, their leashes, any number of odd owner possessions and, rarely, water. I once had a case who compulsively guarded anything within a one-yard radius of his body, including an item – furniture polish – that he was fearful of in other contexts.

11

Combinations

It is not uncommon for the intensity of a dog's guarding to be additive. Consider a dog who is a mild object guarder and moderate bed guarder. If this dog were approached while in possession of a new, coveted toy while on the bed, he would likely demonstrate more severe guarding then ever seen previously. Similarly, body handling issues – or other issues to do with discomfort around strangers or certain strangers - can combine with resource guarding to spike reactions to more severe levels.

Body Handling

Our vision of dogs is filled with images of dogs soliciting patting, and enjoying tummy rubs and ear scratches. And, while we can relate to a dog being nervous or irritable when in pain or when having a scary veterinary procedure done, we are thrown for a loop by dogs who do not relish being touched or handled when our motive is benign or even affectionate. The reality is, however, that we would not expect to easily handle adults of any *other* species of animal if they had not been systematically and extensively handled and gentled as infants and juveniles. This may be bundled with the super high standard we hold dogs to – they should

"naturally" love being touched. The bottom line is that we often drop the ball with puppies by not handling them sufficiently, by omitting certain body parts, by failing to make it pleasant and relaxing for them or, worse, by allowing traumatic experiences to occur and then failing to actively undo the damage.

It's really no surprise then, when you really think about it, that dogs may be defensive and uncomfortable about being touched in certain ways or in certain spots.

The most common handling problems involve:

- Restraint of body, head, jaws and/or limbs
- Collar grabbing
- Head reaches or touches
- Muzzle and mouth
- Ears
- Feet – front only, back only or both
- Nail clipping
- Skin grabbing
- Hair pulling/grooming
- Rear quarters
- Tail

Dog groomers are forced, by the nature of their work, to handle a lot of dogs who are not habituated to being handled. It's no wonder they are so frequently bitten by dogs and that they so often insist, along with many veterinarians, on the use of muzzles. Luckily, although there are many kinds of handling to get a dog used to, well-executed prevention and treatment exercises are straightforward to do and successful in the vast majority of cases.

The Behaviorist and Medical Models

Dog training and behavior modification are fields full of camps with different biases. One well-known distinction is that between trainers who use primarily or exclusively techniques that are free of aversives (e.g. pain and startle) and those who insist that aversives are necessary and benign. Another less well-publicized difference is whether one's focus is on observable data or on interpretations of what might be going on inside the dog's mind. This is the distinction between the behaviorist viewpoint and the medical model. Where a behaviorist is interested in observable and quantifiable behavior, the medical model is oriented toward symptom-diagnosis-treatment.

Where the medical model might see observable behavior as a *symptom* of an underlying problem, syndrome or illness, such as dominance aggression in the case of resource guarding, the behaviorist sticks to what the dog is *doing* – in this case, guarding – and modifies that behavior without attempts at guessing what is going on "in the black box." My very use of the term "resource guarding" belies my bias toward a behaviorist paradigm. I can't know what is going on in the mind of any dog at any time. I can, however, observe, identify, measure and modify behavior using well-established principles of operant and classical conditioning. So, what you find in this manual are descriptions of behavior and techniques for modifying that behavior. This is not to say that I don't have opinions and "gut feelings" or often have an entertaining time speculating about what I *think* is going on in a dog's head. It's just that, when it comes to behavior modification, a focus on what the dog is doing is more fruitful.

Recognizing Guarding

Most guarders will be presented as behaving aggressively to family members rather than strangers. Although many resource guarders will guard from just about anybody who is around, family members are more likely to *be* around enough to come across the behavior. Sometimes the owner will identify that the issue is the dog's control of or proximity to a certain resource, but other times will not know why the dog is being aggressive. It may even appear to a bewildered owner to be completely unpredictable. This is especially likely when there is a hidden combo, or when the resource or body part has simply not been recognized as being "hot."

Questioning will usually reveal that the dog is predictably aggressive when in proximity to his problem resource(s). When taking history, check all the usual suspects: food, objects, locations, owner and body handling. Use novel, high value resources and check using both the owner and yourself. It is likely that the dog is not muzzle-desensitized,

14

and the use of a muzzle on a dog who is not comfortable wearing one could yield a false negative on your tests. For this reason, it's better to use other safety measures, such as Kevlar gloves, a tether and/or an artificial hand.

Assessing Acquired Bite Inhibition

In order to forecast the likely outcome of anti-resource guarding exercises, first and foremost is an assessment of the degree of acquired bite inhibition in the dog. In an overwhelming majority of cases, there will be a static pattern to bite severity, i.e. very little variation within a certain range. For example, if a dog has inflicted five bites of one to four shallow punctures, you can reliably predict that if he were to bite tomorrow, the bite would be of one to four shallow punctures. A hard mouth taking treats is a different kind of hard mouth. It can be modified through operant conditioning, but this seems to have no appreciable effect on the bite severity when the dog bites during resource guarding, handling discomfort or when fearful. There are to date no effective techniques to address the latter kind of hard mouth.

To assess bite severity, the first order of business is to obtain a thorough history of all the dog's bites to people and other dogs, including all fights or squabbles with other dogs. The most important feature is the degree of damage per bite. It may require some sleuthing to extract this information from the flood of other details you may experience during history taking, such as the context in which bites occurred, immediate triggers, the owner's perception about the triggers (i.e. their emotional reaction to whether the bite was warranted or sufficiently "provoked"), other threat signals present and the owner's perception about the dog's apparent motivation, intention and state of mind. Do not be distracted from your task of finding out precisely, for each incident, exactly what kind of injury occurred to what person on what body part through what kind of clothing and what, if any, medical attention they received.

15

Many other history aspects will be highly relevant later on, for determining triggers, designing hierarchies and for management, but for the purpose of assessing bite inhibition, you must edit these out for now. If the bite inhibition is abysmally poor, for instance, it may render the case untreatable. You will want, as soon as possible, to give the client some sense of whether you think you can help them or not. Also, your immediate case management and "damage control" recommendations to the client will depend to a large degree on what you discover about bite inhibition. This is why you must tease this aspect out first when taking history.

Many trainers believe that a dogfight history may yield some insight about bite inhibition. I would caution that this information is not as predictive as a bite history. Interviewing for this information must again be directed at bite inhibition, which can get obscured by the other fight elements that seem relevant to an upset owner. The cleanest, most highly ritualized dogfights are dramatic looking and can be very distressing for owners to witness. Your client's dog may have himself been injured (which speaks to the other dog's bite inhibition, which is not relevant), victimized or been an apparent instigator. Once again, your sole interest is in the degree of damage inflicted on the other dog and nature of veterinary attention he may have received.

There is no absolute standard regarding what kind of bite severity equates a treatable case. It is a judgment call made by the counselor prior to deciding to treat aggression cases. Many qualified trainers and behaviorists opt to not take on aggression at all. Some will only treat cases where there is minimal (e.g. shallow abrasions to an occasional shallow puncture) or no damage, or cases where the dog gives all manner of protracted threat but has not bitten anyone due to a gloriously high bite threshold. Others may treat anything up to single bites with four moderate punctures but without any bi-directional tearing (bites where the dog held and shook, causing tearing in two directions from the points of initial puncture). And some counselors will treat all kinds of mouths, though they may examine other history features – the owner's management capabilities, potential liability and presence of children in the home - before committing. My personal recommendation is strong management or euthanasia for dogs who inflict deep punctures and contusions with or without bi-directional tearing.

The important thing is that you decide what you feel comfortable and qualified to counsel on before fielding inquiries, and that you refer appropriately when you encounter a case that falls outside your scope.

When assessing bite severity, the nature and clothing of the victim and where on the victim's body the bite occurred are relevant. The amount of jaw pressure that might produce mild bruising on an adult man's calf through denim might seriously disfigure a child's face. Similarly, an ear rip inflicted during a dogfight may bleed dramatically and a Whippet might be punctured extremely easily, but the same amount of pressure would have produced zero damage on most dogs on most other body parts. Finally, in general, most dogs do not puncture as easily as most humans. Bear all these distinctions in mind when taking a bite inhibition history.

When there are no bites on record, some information about mouth can be gleaned by finding out about the dog's play history with other dogs (soft jaw-wrestling is what you're after here – chase play has no bearing), mouthing (play-biting) history with humans, the dog's apparent prudence in situations where the owner has had their hands in the dog's mouth (such as during tooth-brushing or pilling) and, finally, the roughness when taking treats. Be advised, however, that these indicators are far less reliable than a true bite history. I usually use them as supplementary evidence when there is a limited though favorable bite history on record.

It should be reiterated that although there seems to be some sketchy correlation between the hardness of a dog's mouth when taking treats, having teeth cared for and play-mouthing and the hardness of a dog's mouth when the chips are down, the former can be modified but there is no evidence that it has any bearing on bite severity during resource guarding.

When there is paltry or no information about the dog's degree of bite inhibition, it is safest to proceed as though the mouth were poor and employ a muzzle for the early trips up the hierarchy and strong management and situational awareness between sessions.

Other Prognostic Indicators

The other factors that have a bearing on the likelihood of successful resolution are:

- ❑ Number and clarity of triggers
- ❑ Owner commitment and compliance
- ❑ Bite threshold and presence of protracted warning
- ❑ Dog variables such as impulsivity, size and learning ability

There is little question that a dog who guards his food bowl during his dinner and possibly a couple of other high value items is a simpler dog to fix than one who guards his food bowl and other food items, and certain toys, and novel and forbidden objects and is a little tricky to groom. How well defined the triggers are is also a factor. A dog who religiously guards the bed from dad and is iffy when dad tries to move him off the sofa is a rosier prospect than one who guards in many situations and whose behavior to the same stimulus is not predictable. These "fuzzy" or hard to pin down triggers make the design of a desensitization hierarchy, not to mention management between sessions, very tricky. The likelihood of nailing down exactly what the problem is and preventing re-offense during treatment is worse than for dogs with well-defined triggers.

Ian Dunbar has said that the owner variable is enormous in dog training. He is absolutely right. Severe and refractory cases in the hands of a capable and committed owner are often a better bet than relatively mild cases owned by people with low skill and low motivation. One of the factors  implicated in trainer burnout is a steady stream of cases that would be routine fixes if only the owner were up to the program. A promising development in our profession is an influx of trainers and behavior counselors with better people skills and knowledge of how to instruct, educate and motivate adult learners. This can only increase our batting average with cases where the owner variable may be a weak link.

Every dog, when defending resources has a characteristic threat signature. Some will do a classic sequence of first freezing up, then growling, then snarling, snapping and finally, if these all fail, biting, hopefully in an inhibited fashion. Other dogs give very little in the way of protracted warning – they seem fine and then explosively bite. Most dogs lie somewhere in the middle. What threat signals a dog gives, what kind of delays there are between them and how intense an approaching threat must be to finally elicit a bite make up this signature.

The ideal treatment prospect will have a high bite threshold, multiple levels of clear threat and a relatively slow escalation to each successive threat level. This way, whether during treatment exercises or a real life encounter, there is plenty of advertisement from the dog that he may bite the approacher. Contrast this with the dog with a low bite threshold and no protracted warning. Rather than biting you when you're literally on top of him grappling for the resource, and this after he froze, growled and snarled in succession during your approach, the low threshold/no warning dog demonstrates no change in behavior and then suddenly bites you when you bend over slightly from three feet away to see what he has.

Learning rate is another prognostic indicator. Although I think the concept of dog intelligence is over-played, there are clear learning rate differences between dogs. In many cases these can be traced to a more enriched environment, particularly when a dog has been taught other things and is benefiting from a "learning to learn" effect. In other cases, it could be a natural facility with learning in general or of learning anti-resource guarding type tasks in particular. Dogs who learn better will move more quickly up hierarchies, all other things being equal.

There seems to be a quality in some dogs that is not learning rate, but rather something that interferes with an otherwise normal ability to learn. For lack of a better description, I'll label it impulsivity – a tendency for the dog to respond in what appears to be a more reflexive and emotional way. When this is present in a resource guarder, it will slow progress down. This may be one factor that is affected by the use of some medications.

Finally, it is an unavoidable truth that the size of the dog is directly correlated with the degree of damage he can inflict, as well as the perception of the severity of any aggression problem by both the owner and society at large. So, size impacts compliance as well as liability risk and so will in turn impact treatment outcome statistics.

Use of Muzzles and Tethers

There are advantages and disadvantages to the use of any tool in behavior modification. One disadvantage is always the necessity of fading or weaning off the tool unless dependence on it in real life situations is immaterial and the tool can always be at hand. In the case of resource guarding, muzzles and tethers provide safety during exercises, especially in those cases where a super-threshold mishap could result in a bite from a dog with a moderate or poor mouth. They are often used in early exercises until the dog is well rehearsed. Then, they are dispensed with so the training can be generalized to increasingly real life situations.

I would advise the use of a muzzle, tether or possibly heavy gloves (such as Kevlar) in the early stages of work with dogs with known damaging mouths as well as with dogs whose degree of bite inhibition is not known. The other time I recommend muzzles and tethers is when children in the family are doing exercises, even if the mouth is good. Muzzles are problematic during food bowl exercises, as the dog cannot consume the kibble, so in this case, a tether and/or use of gloves are standard defensive precautions.

The standard procedure is to work up a hierarchy with the dog muzzle and/or tethered, achieving reliability on cold trials. Cold trials are the first trial of any training session, before the dog is "warmed up." These are key landmarks as there is often a dramatic difference in response when a dog is in the middle of a session versus the first response of the first session of the day, which is much more like real life. Once the dog is reliable for cold trials muzzled, the hierarchy is repeated in its entirety without the muzzle.

When there are children in the family, the dog should be taken up the hierarchy (including cold trial success) on muzzle by adults, then on muzzle by any kids, then off muzzle by adults and, finally, off muzzle by the kids. Or, after going up on muzzle with the adults, go up off muzzle with the adults, then back on muzzle with all kids and then off muzzle with the kids. The most important thing is that the kids are only doing exercises off muzzle once the dog has been up the hierarchy three times successfully with adults. By this stage, the response is strong, well generalized and the likelihood of surprises the smallest.

Tethers impede lunging, and so I especially recommend them in cases of poor protracted warning, low bite threshold, unknown warning or threshold, or when trying to get a better diagnostic handle on fuzzy triggers. As with muzzles, ensure you have reliability on cold trials on the tether before re-initiating the hierarchy off the tether. Unlike muzzles, tethers do not require any pre-desensitization in order to use them.

The best kind of muzzle to use for resource guarding exercises is a tube-shaped groomer's muzzle, mainly because it allows for easier treat delivery than a basket muzzle. Palatable treats are the perfect choice for counterconditioning in most cases of resource guarding. Basket muzzles allow panting, but not very easy delivery of treats. Because you will be using a tube muzzle, the dog should not be worked in hot weather, right after heavy physical exertion. If you suspect he is hot and needs to pant, take a break in the session.

Muzzle Desensitization

Before using the muzzle during exercises, it should be introduced to the dog in a systematic way, in order to minimize the amount it slows down the eventual generalized response. It is also less aversive than just slapping one on the dog.   Here is a sample hierarchy for muzzle desensitization and counterconditioning. Do not progress to the next step in the program until you have achieved the goal on the current step. You can expect to spend a week or two completing all the steps if you work at least once a day for 15-20 minutes.

I. Show the dog the muzzle and then give him a generous handful of tasty treats – repeat this several times per day until he is demonstrating a happy, anticipatory response when he sees the muzzle, very much like the response dogs have when they see their leash come out of the closet.

II. Play a targeting game with the muzzle wherein you hold out the muzzle and reward the dog every time he bumps it with his nose. A clicker trained dog is a plus here to mark nice responses. For information on clicker training, see Karen Pryor's wonderful book *Don't Shoot the Dog!*

III. When the dog is targeting as quickly as you can present the muzzle, reward only after every two or three nose bumps. While doing so, try to select the nose bumps that are a little longer and stronger.

IV. Hold the muzzle with the entrance to the nose tube facing the dog. Reward him for getting his nose anywhere in that area now. Give especially large rewards when he does any approximation of putting his nose right in. It's okay to prompt responses at this stage by holding a treat at the other end so that the dog must insert his nose in order to collect through the tube. It is sometimes okay to leap right in with this prompting exercise, skipping parts I – III, but the most prudent course of action is to spend a bit of time with the preliminary exercises.

V. The reward standard is now the dog putting his nose right into the muzzle. If you have achieved this with prompting, fade the prompt now so that the dog must put his nose in *before* you produce the treat rather than putting his nose in once the treat is visible at the end.

VI. Add duration to step V. Once the dog's nose is in the muzzle, delay giving the reward through the hole for a second or two. Praise him lavishly while he waits. Tell him how attractive he looks. Gradually increase the time he must remain in the muzzle up to 10 seconds.

VII. Adjust the muzzle straps so that they would fit him extremely loosely. While he is waiting in the muzzle for his treat, as per step VI, start fiddling with the head straps while he waits. When he is used to this, try snapping the muzzle on very loosely. Praise him for all you're worth the first time you attach it and feed him generously. When you first start messing with the straps, he may withdraw his nose for a while – if he does, back off temporarily and then try again with more subtle strap-fiddling.

VIII. Adjust the muzzle straps so that they are closer to a correct fit (which is snugly around the back of his head, right up under the occiput, the pointy bone at the back of his head). Snap the muzzle on and give him extra praise and food rewards again. He is so handsome.

IX. Gradually tighten the fit and extend the duration for which he wears the muzzle. Now you are ready to employ it during anti-guarding and handling exercises.

Treatment Overview

A typical resource guarding rehabilitation program will center on direct desensitization and counterconditioning exercises to modify any known guarding. Great attention will be paid in most cases to getting the new behavior generalized so that the dog is safe around people in general, rather than only those who have done exercises. Adjunct measures, such as impulse control exercises, the provision of vigorous exercise and mental stimulation, and coaching the owner about animal learning principles are also common. Remember to always perform a thorough check of all other guarding types than the one initially presented, and check for body handling. If these are present, or if there are other behavior issues you have been engaged to work on, discuss these with the family and then compose a priority list of what will be done in what order. Include your prognosis estimate for the various problems to help the owners set appropriate expectations.

Sometimes more than one target problem can be worked on at once and sometimes it's better to focus on one thing at a time, perhaps initiating adjunct exercises or changes to the dog's routine immediately as well. Prior to exercises, you will have desensitized the dog to wearing a muzzle if you have opted to use one. You will have considered any possible adjuncts to the desensitization and counterconditioning exercises, such as changes to the dog's routine and training, exercise and recommendations regarding how family members might better interact with him. And, you will have explained the program to the family, including the necessity of managing the dog's environment throughout the program.

Management

Management means avoiding the problem or trigger for a behavior through environmental control. It can serve as a valid alternative to behavior modification sometimes or be used in conjunction with behavior modification. Managing during treatment serves the dual purposes of preventing mishap while the dog is in training and protecting the program. For instance, if an object guarder has been worked part way up a hierarchy so that he is reliable for rawhides but has not yet had exercises addressing pigs' ears, an ill-fated confrontation over a pigs' ear one day could set progress back even with rawhides. The first line of defense for managing a resource guarder is to purge the dog's environment of all items he has not yet mastered in exercises. Think of it as hiding all the grade 12 quizzes from the grade 8 student (until he has passed grade 12).

This is not always possible to do, so the other line of defense is to avoid confrontation should a situation arise that is too advanced for the dog's current level. An example would be a bed-guarder who has been barred from the bedroom in between training exercises as he is not yet ready for cold or spontaneous trials. If, one day, the bedroom door is left open and the dog gets on the bed, the owner should simply ignore the dog and wait for him to come off the bed on his own. An alternative is a simple re-direction. In a very matter of fact way, call the dog to the kitchen for a cookie or invite him out for a brief walk.

If the situation is an emergency – such as when an object guarder gets hold of something truly dangerous on the street, which can't be ignored, first try a "bait and switch." Quickly and calmly bribe or distract the dog with anything you can think of. If the dog has a history of this sort of guarding, it is a good idea to pack a fabulous emergency item for just such purposes. This is infinitely less dangerous and harmful than attempting to confront, reprimand or wrestle. Although bribery is totally ineffective for fostering actual behavior change, when you're in a jam, anything goes. Jams are not training situations. All you're after at that moment is to get out of the jam with the least damage done to owner, dog and training program. Again, careful management prevents jams.

Special Considerations for Children

The presence of children in the home changes the resource guarding or body-handling picture. Young kids have a hard time complying with management rules, innocently toddling up to dogs. Their stature makes any bite more likely to be to the face. For these reasons, the bar must be higher when kids are present. Consider placing the dog in an adult only home or even euthanasia if the dog's mouth is not good or the bite threshold low. As stated earlier, the dog should be muzzled for kids' first trips up the hierarchy, and should follow completed trips by all adults. And, finally, kids need to be coached during training sessions by a competent adult.

Principles of Desensitization
and Counterconditioning

Systematic desensitization is a technique that was originally developed by behavioral psychologists to treat people with anxiety and phobias. The subject is exposed to a fear-evoking object or situation at an intensity that does not produce a response. If you were terrified of ants, for example, your first hierarchy rung might involve showing you a cartoon of a pink, unrealistic ant, at a distance if necessary. You wouldn't be the slightest bit afraid (hopefully). The intensity - in this case, degree of realism and proximity - is then very gradually increased contingent upon the subject continuing to feel okay. A hierarchy is developed at the beginning of treatment, ranging from the easiest to most difficult level versions of the stimulus.

Desensitization is most often performed in conjunction with another technique, *counterconditioning*, which is an application of classical or Pavlovian conditioning. In classical conditioning, when one event becomes a reliable predictor of another event, the subject develops an anticipatory response to the first event. The association between the two events is particularly evident if the second event is relevant or potent.

There are important advantages for animals of learning the tip-offs to important environmental events. Dogs learn that a leash coming out of the cupboard means a walk is next. Cats learn that the sound of the can opener means food is next. And we all know the story of Pavlov's dogs.

What if, whenever I show you the picture of the ant, I then give you a bit of favorite Belgian chocolate? With repetition, you will start to have a nice feeling about that ant.

It's crucial to maintain the distinction between classical and operant conditioning. In classical conditioning the animal is learning about events and their predictive relationship with other events. In operant conditioning he is learning about his own voluntary behavior and its consequences. Classical conditioning is about associations. Operant conditioning is about rewards and punishments. And, the anticipatory response that is conditioned using classical conditioning procedures is involuntary.

All kinds of involuntary responses can be classically conditioned, such as gastric and salivary secretions, immune responses and autonomic reflexes. These are of little practical interest in dog behavior modification, but *emotional* responses are of tremendous interest. Pairing one stimulus with a meaningful second stimulus can create a Conditioned Emotional Response, or CER. Many of the original CER experiments involved the conditioning of fear responses by pairing otherwise neutral or positive things with aversive, scary things. We are usually interested in making dogs feel *good* rather than bad about certain events, however, so instead of using aversives to condition, we use things the dog really, really likes, such as tasty food, toys or walks.

Counterconditioning is about changing associations. It's called *counter*conditioning rather than simply conditioning because the dog already has an unpleasant emotional response to the thing we're trying to condition, so we *counter* that by establishing a pleasant CER. So, where a food guarder used to feel tense and upset when a person approached him while eating, after conditioning he loves and looks forward to being approached while eating.

How this looks in actual treatment is the presentation of a low-enough intensity, or *sub-threshold*, version of the trigger, immediately followed by a potent, pleasant counter-conditioning stimulus. This is repeated until the dog is evidently and eagerly anticipating the counter-stimulus when the trigger is presented. Then, the intensity of the trigger is increased and the procedure repeated. If, at any point, the dog shows the original reaction to the trigger, it means the intensity of the presentation is *super*-threshold. It is important to then back off to a reduced trigger intensity and work back up gradually again. No good comes of rehearsing the dog's old, growly behavior by replicating super-threshold versions of the trigger. In fact, it can make the dog worse. Here's how to apply desensitization and counterconditioning (D&C) principles to resource guarders.

Hierarchy Construction

Once you have ascertained what the dog guards – food, objects, locations, owner etc. – the next step is drafting initial hierarchy rungs for your D&C sessions. This will mean interviewing the owner and possibly auditioning items yourself. List items that the dog does not guard and those that he does. Items from the unguarded list are used in early exercises to teach the dog the game at a guaranteed sub-threshold level. If possible, divide items on the guarded list into high, medium and lower value. Often these lists will be firmed up once you begin working on the dog in earnest.

In the interest of being thorough, be sure to consider common items in the guarded category that the dog may not yet have encountered. Object guarders may have histories with pigs' ears and tennis balls but have never encountered marrow bones or plush toys. It's impossible to be completely exhaustive, but a generalized response – i.e. the dog is now safe with novel items and/or in novel situations – is a goal of treatment and the more bases you cover, the closer you will get to that nice, strong yet elusive generalized response.

If the dog has a known hard mouth or an unknown mouth, use precautions when testing. As you will have to perform muzzle desensitization anyway for exercises, you have the option of doing the muzzle desensitization first and then testing likely items. Or, test items using Kevlar gloves, a tether and/or an artificial hand if you wish to have this fleshed out before commencing muzzle desensitization.

On the next page are lists of typical items to check for.

Food Guarding Auditioning Checklist

Empty bowl – mealtime and random time
Regular kibble
Mix of canned food and kibble
Canned food
Bait used in training
High value food items – to simulate steals or treats
Stuffed Kongs
Any guarded food item reported by the owner

Object Guarding Auditioning Checklist

Latex squeaky toys
Balls
Sticks
Plush toys
Kleenexes
Rawhides and Pig's ears
Marrow bones and butcher bones
Illegal items such as kids' toys, laundry, soiled diapers
Any guarded object reported by the owner

Location Guarding Auditioning Checklist

Dog's bed(s)
Sofa(s) and chair(s)
Beds of family members
Crate
Car
Favorite or enclosed spots, such as under or behind furniture
Any guarded location reported by the owner

Variables

The nature of the item is not the only factor that determines stimulus intensity and attendant level of difficulty. The distance one approaches the dog from and the angle of approach can be factors. In general, the further away you are approaching from, the worse the guarding once you get to the dog's guarding radius. The other end of this continuum is a sharing scenario, such as holding onto a rawhide while the dog chews it. When you do not totally relinquish possession yourself, the dog's guarding is usually attenuated. Some guarders are so severe that you may need to begin, or begin for certain items, with you in close proximity to the item and at a distance from the tethered dog, flipping him his counterconditioning prize in each trial.

Some dogs are more sensitive to angle of approach than others, flaring up differentially if approached from the front, the side, or the rear. If the dog is sensitive to this factor, take note of it, as you must cover those bases. It will also give you another variable to juggle when you are stumped on other parameters. Many dogs are very likely to be sensitive to your orientation – whether you are facing them square on and making eye contact, or whether you are at an indirect angle and not looking right at them. Again, this is a variable to juggle and a base to cover.

How long the dog has had possession is often a significant factor. In most cases, a dog will be more likely to guard when he has had possession for long enough to get "dug in." Occasional dogs will flare up on initial possession and then, when the novelty wears off and their interest flags, are less likely to guard. Novel items are usually implicated in this latter case.

Who's doing the approach also matters. Dogs are great at discriminating fine differences. They easily learn such things as whom it is safe or dangerous to jump up on, who is likely to be packing rewards for obedience etc. Dogs are not great natural generalizers. They do not automatically transfer responses they have learned with one person to other people.

In anti-resource guarding training, it often takes a handful or more people to actually do exercises in order to see the conditioned response with new people who have not participated in exercises. This difference will be augmented if the dog is not well socialized to a particular category of people. For instance, if a dog is not perfectly comfortable with men, he will likely regress dramatically when men do exercises with him. Many instances of flared up resource guarding are caused by such added factors.

The last variable that can affect stimulus and therefore

guarding intensity is how warmed up the dog is. Is it the first trial of the training session or have you been practicing for 20 minutes and done 50 trials already? Very often you will make progress as you do repetitions in a session but the peak you achieve will not translate into performance on a spontaneous or "cold" trial. This is something because even though the dog may be steadily successful at a certain level in training sessions, if he were to encounter that same level suddenly in real life, he may still guard, as the trained response is still dependent on warm-up. It usually takes longer to make a dog reliable on cold trials, but it is not an insurmountable obstacle, just another base to cover. The maxim is: if he can do it warmed up, he can do it cold; it's just a matter of time.

In addition to auditioning items and getting a handle on the other variables discussed, it behooves you to audition the kinds of bait you plan to use as counterconditioning stimuli. There is little point in attempting to condition a CER using something the dog is lukewarm about. The dog may have a clear hierarchy of different kinds of bait, which is useful to know. For example, diced hot dogs may be exciting but can be trumped by Liver Biscotti, which in turn can be trumped by diced cheddar. Sometimes, even if there is no clear winner but the dog is besotted with more than one kind of bait, it's a smart strategy to rotate these treats so they retain some of the extra kick of novelty. If there is a clear hierarchy, reserve the very highest levels for trickier rungs on the hierarchy, such as when exchanging for higher value objects or removing higher value food.

Execution of D&C Exercises

I cannot count the number of times I've heard people announce that a certain technique – operant conditioning for example – "didn't work" in a given case. Of course it could be that the technique was not a good choice for the task, but the first rule-out is usually execution errors. In other words, although someone thinks they're doing procedure X and not getting anywhere, they are actually committing compromising or even lethal technical errors that, if resolved, would allow progress. In the case of D & C, it is vital to thoroughly understand the principles and then to execute properly in order to get a good result.

Rehearsals

In order to start conditioning at solidly sub-threshold level, the first exercise is always rehearsal on dummy items, or is performed out of context. This is known as teaching the dog the game. Here are suggested first rungs for the different guarding types.

Object guarder:	Exchanges with zero-value (non-guarded) objects, or, if dog compulsively guards anything,
	Exchanges with lowest value objects at a distance – dog on tether - that evokes no guarding reaction
Food guarder:	Installment feeding to empty food bowl up close or,
	Approaches to empty food bowl in order to feed in installments
Location guarder:	Placement exercises out of context (at times when dog is not interested in claiming location) or, if dog always compulsively guards location,
	Placement exercises using unguarded furniture or props
Owner guarder:	Approaches to owner with dog on

tether to a distance away that evokes
no guarding

The objective of this initial exercise is to train the Conditioned Emotional Response (CER). Be sure to explain this groundwork to the owner and that you will be getting to the guarding scenarios in due course. Otherwise, he or she may feel that you're not really working on the problem and shortchange the essential preparation. Each dog's CER, once established, will be unique. In most cases it will involve a happy facial expression, some eager checking of where the bait usually comes from and possibly tail-wagging or other signs of hopeful anticipation. Trainers often call this response the "yippee" response. It's the dog's expression of recognition that the good stuff is on the way.

Rehearse the first exercise until there is a clear yippee response on approach, exchange or, in the case of placement exercises, when the cue is initiated. In this last case, the yippee response will be occurring as the dog performs the behavior (i.e. moving to where you have indicated) and will sometimes translate into a snappy, happy looking response, very much the way a dog looks when executing a favorite trick for a treat.

Order of Events in Classical Conditioning

The difference between establishing a beautiful CER and literally achieving nothing is very often due to how well the trainer orchestrates the order of events. If you remember, in order for a dog to have an anticipatory response to the first event in a classical conditioning procedure, it must have high predictive value that the second event is coming. This predictive relationship can be muddied by a couple of common errors.

First, there is a risk of simultaneous or backward conditioning. Simultaneous conditioning refers to presentations where the second event occurs simultaneous to the first, so there is no predictive relationship. Backward conditioning refers to presentations of the two events in reverse order so that the predictive relationship is also reversed. Dogs get excited at the sight of their leash coming out of the cupboard because the walk comes *afterwards*. If the walk happened simultaneous to or before the leash came out of the cupboard, the leash's appearance would not be a very good tip-off. It wouldn't give the dog any information about when a walk is coming.

Similarly, if events in a resource counterconditioning procedure are not in the correct order, conditioning won't take place. The first event is the approach or other "threat" to the resource (such as, in later exercises, touching it, removing it or touching the dog while he is in possession). The second event is the fabulous pay-off, along with the dog retaining the original resource or getting it back.

In an object exchange, this means that the approach, touch or removal of the object must *precede* the delivery of the counterconditioning treat. Similarly, in a food bowl exercise, the approach, bowl touch or bowl removal must precede the addition of bonuses to the dish. If the trainer is trying to "prevent" a guarding reaction by showing the dog the bait up front, or if the order of presentation gets sloppy, the emotional response either will not get conditioned or will get conditioned, but to something other than the approach and/or removal. Also, many people feel intuitively that if events are close together in time, animals will form associations regardless of the precise order of events, but this is a mistaken intuition. On the next pages, consider the comparisons of standard, simultaneous and backward pairings (time moves from left to right).

Establishment of a CER to the appearance of a leash

LEASH

WALK

Yippee! **CONDITIONED RESPONSE TO LEASH**

Simultaneous Conditioning

LEASH

WALK

NO RESPONSE TO LEASH POST CONDITIONING

Backward Conditioning

LEASH

WALK

NO RESPONSE TO LEASH POST CONDITIONING

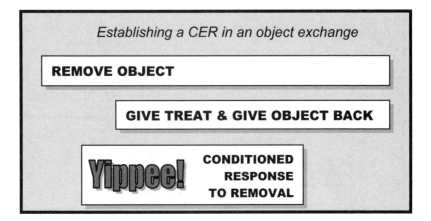

Establishing a CER in an object exchange

REMOVE OBJECT

GIVE TREAT & GIVE OBJECT BACK

Yippee! **CONDITIONED RESPONSE TO REMOVAL**

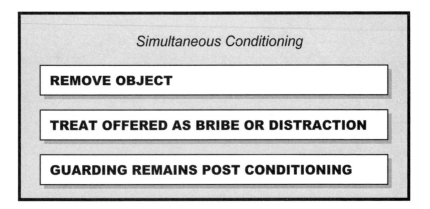

Simultaneous Conditioning

REMOVE OBJECT

TREAT OFFERED AS BRIBE OR DISTRACTION

GUARDING REMAINS POST CONDITIONING

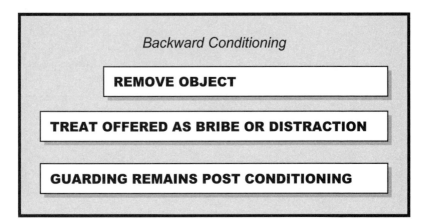

Backward Conditioning

REMOVE OBJECT

TREAT OFFERED AS BRIBE OR DISTRACTION

GUARDING REMAINS POST CONDITIONING

Establishing a CER to a food bowl approach

APPROACH BOWL

DELIVER BAIT OR FEEDING INSTALLMENT

Yippee! **CONDITIONED RESPONSE TO APPROACH**

Simultaneous Conditioning

APPROACH BOWL

VISIBLY OFFER BAIT OR HANDFUL

NO CER TO APPROACH

Backward Conditioning

APPROACH BOWL

VISIBLY OFFER BAIT OR HANDFUL

NO CER TO APPROACH

Another common order of events snafu is the CER latching onto some other element in the stimulus package preceding the bait delivery other than the element you want: the approach, touch or removal. This could be the training context itself. If trials are delivered in too rapid fire a manner from the beginning to the end of the session without any down time, the dog might develop a stronger or exclusive CER to the exercise set-up and/or to the trainer. If trials are delivered in too steady a manner, the inter-trial interval can actually overshadow the approach. What this means is the dog learns a rule such as "treats are arriving every eight seconds" rather than attending to the approach or exchange that precedes the treat. Finally, if some other thing the dog is already familiar with as a predictor of good stuff – such as the smell of the bait or the reach of the trainer's hand toward's the bait pouch – occurs simultaneous to the approach, touch or removal, that element could block what you are trying to condition.

These things are potentially better predictors to the dog of the good stuff, so it is well worth the effort to explicitly rule them out. The goal is to counteract an existing response to approach, touch or removal of a resource, so it is critical that the new CER is to this and not to something else. Once you've lined up your order of presentation ducks, pay attention to ruling yourself and the overall training context out as an alternative predictor. An efficient way to do this is to spend time with the dog, in the location you will work, carrying the bait on you that you will use in exercises, but without doing any exercises. This way the dog experiences your presence and the smell of the bait but without having any delivered. This time can be during actual training sessions – dead time – and/or at other times. The key thing is that the only event that reliably predicts that the delicious goodies are coming is the approach, touch or removal of the resource.

Predictability

Another factor that will influence the strength of conditioning is the correlation between the bait you're using and the resource removal (or approach and touch). If the exercises sometimes occur without the bait or the bait sometimes is given without the exercise, the correlation will be lower and the strength of your CER compromised. For this reason, don't be tempted to do exercises with low value treats for convenience on occasion and don't use the high value bait you're using in D&C exercises for other training endeavors or as general dog treats. Reserve it for its sole purpose.

Sample Hierarchies

The following are examples of hierarchies. Each case is slightly different, and you will sail through certain portions and get bogged down at others. The slow parts will be due to the dog guarding. When this happens, you must go back to the step you were last successful on and design intermediate steps between this and the problematic step. Often this will involve juggling the variables we discussed earlier: distances between dog, resource and trainer, how long the dog has had possession, your angle of approach and orientation while approaching and how warmed up the dog is.

Advance to the next step only when there is absolutely no guarding evident at the current step; the dog is comfortable and demonstrating his version of the "yippee" response on each trial, including cold trials (first trial of the session or random one-trial spot checks), if applicable. This is known as skating on thick, rather than thin, ice. Sometimes this will mean just a handful of trials at a given step, and other times it may mean much more repetition or the insertion of intermediate steps when guarding crops up.

Unlike in operant conditioning, longer sessions are usually

more fruitful for desensitizing resource guarders. Aim to do sessions of at least 30 minutes with as many trials as you can manage, given the necessity of breaking up the session with "dead air" to rule you and your smelly bait out as predictors. In food guarding, when you are at the stage where the dog is consuming food, your session length will be limited by how long it takes the dog to consume his ration. It sometimes pays to use obstacles in the bowl (tennis balls, rocks, rubber rings, even taping food down) to slow him down in order to squeeze out more repetitions.

Each step will require at least several repetitions before you see a clear "yippee!" response, with some steps even requiring more than one session. Never move on to the next step until the dog is well conditioned at the current step – this means a nice, solid "yippee!" and no evidence of guarding.

Food Bowl Guarding Sample Hierarchy

Level One: Empty Food Bowl

If the dog guards the food bowl when empty, begin the hierarchy with an approach to a distance 10 feet from the bowl followed by food tosses toward the bowl. Decrease distance by a couple of feet as the dog is successful. If the dog does not guard an empty bowl, begin with Step 1. If the dog guards regardless of distance from the empty bowl, get a new bowl and start practicing with that in a different location from the dog's usual meal location and at a different time from the dog's usual meal time.

If the dog's bite inhibition is unknown, tether the dog during exercises and wear Kevlar gloves until all hierarchy levels have been successfully completed. Then recommence the hierarchy without tether and gloves.

Step 1:   Approach dog and his empty bowl from 6 feet away, drop treats in bowl, then walk away and repeat. Include approaches from different angles, vary the interval between approaches and incorporate long pauses occasionally where you are present but there are no approaches and no treats given

Step 2: Approach from 10 feet, drop treats in empty bowl, then walk away. Include approaches from different angles etc.

Step 3: Approach from 20 feet, drop treats in empty bowl, walk away. Etc.

Step 4: Approach from 10 feet and bend 1/2 of the distance to the bowl as if to pick it up. Drop treats in and walk away

Step 5: Approach from 10 feet and bend all the way toward the bowl as if to pick it up, stopping with treat hand an inch or so from bowl. Drop treats in and walk away

Step 6: Approach from 10 feet, bend over as if to pick up bowl with treat hand, pause 2 seconds, then drop treats in and walk away

Step 7: Proof random distances and angles of approach, with 2 second pause and treat drop

Step 8: Approach from 10 feet, reach toward bowl but do not actually pick it up, then drop treats in bowl with opposite hand

Step 9: Approach from 10 feet, reach toward bowl and touch it for 1 second, then add treats to the bowl with the opposite hand

Step 10: Approach from 10 feet, touch bowl for 3

seconds, then add treats with the opposite hand

Step 11:   Approach and touch for 5 seconds before adding treats with opposite hand

Step 12:   Approach and touch for 10 seconds before adding treats with opposite hand

Step 13:   Approach and touch for 20 seconds before adding treats with opposite hand

Step 14:   Approach and touch for 30 seconds before adding treats with opposite hand

Step 15:   Proof random distances and angles of approach with 30-second bowl-touch prior to treat addition with opposite hand

Step 16:   Approach, grasp and move bowl around for 2 seconds, then add treats with opposite hand

Step 17:   Approach, grasp and move bowl around for 5 seconds, then add treats with opposite hand

Step 18:   Approach, grasp and move bowl around for 10 seconds, then add treats with opposite hand

Step 19:   Approach and lift up empty bowl to waist level, add treats and return bowl

Step 20:   Approach and take away empty food bowl to a counter or table, add treats and return bowl

If the dog has no body handling issues, proceed to step 21. If handling issues are present, these must be formally addressed before progressing to step 21.

Step 21:   Approach, pat the dog's back for 1 second, then add treats to bowl with opposite hand

Step 22:   Approach, pat the dog's back for 3 seconds, then add treats to bowl with opposite hand

Step 23:   Approach, pat the dog's back for 5 seconds, then add treats to bowl with opposite hand

Step 24:   Approach, pat the dog's back for 1-2 seconds, take bowl away, add treats, return bowl

Step 25:   Proof random distances and angles

Level Two: Beginning with Step 1, complete the above hierarchy using dry kibble in the food bowl – remember to approach and add something more palatable than the dry kibble

Level Three: Beginning with Step 1, complete the above hierarchy using an approximately 50% dry and 50% canned food mixture instead of just dry kibble - remember to approach and add something more palatable

Level Four: Beginning with Step 1, complete the above hierarchy using canned food instead of the dry/wet food mixture - remember to approach and add something more palatable

Level Five: Beginning with Step 1, complete the above hierarchy using a solidly frozen roast or frozen chicken in the bowl – if there is nothing obviously more palatable, approach and add the tastiest bits from another chicken or roast, which you can prepare beforehand. You may also be able to trump the resource with defrosted chicken or roast with gravy on it

Maintenance consists of occasional spot checks, which are bowl touches or removals with bonus additions. If there is ever any small sign of guarding, this will be tidied up. We'll discuss maintenance and regressions in more detail later.

Object Guarding Sample Hierarchy

Object guarders are slightly more complicated than dogs who guard strictly their food bowl, as there are often more guarding contexts and items to cover. Here's how to proceed.

If the dog compulsively guards any object, tether him to practice exchanges on the lowest possible value object 10 feet away, flipping him his treat after you pick up the object at your feet. If there are unguarded objects, begin with Step 1.

If the dog's bite inhibition is unknown, desensitize the dog to a muzzle before doing any exercises with items the dog has ever guarded. Once you have successfully completed the hierarchy on muzzle, re-initiate off muzzle. You can also have the dog on a tether for the first trip up the hierarchy.

If you are having difficulty keeping the dog near unguarded objects - he wanders away and no longer is in close enough proximity to simulate "possession" - tether him or put him on a down-stay if he is comfortable doing one. If his down-stay was originally installed using aversives, or is unreliable, I recommend the tether to avoid mishap and any false negatives elicited by old associations with corrections.

Step 1:   Approach dog and unguarded object from 6 feet away, take object away, deliver treat from pouch or from behind back with opposite hand, give object back, walk away, then repeat. Include approaches from different angles, vary the interval between approaches and incorporate long pauses occasionally where you are present but there are no approaches and no treats

Step 2:   Approach from 10 feet, take object away, deliver treat, give object back, then walk away. Include approaches from different angles etc.

Step 3:   Approach from 20 feet, take object away etc.

If the dog has no body handling issues, proceed to step 4. If he does, work on these before advancing to step 4.

Step 4:   Approach from 10 feet, pat dog's back for 1-2 seconds, then take object away etc.

Step 5:   Approach from 10 feet, pat dog's back for 5 seconds, then take object away etc.

Step 6:   Tether dog if you have done the preceding steps off tether, and sit a couple of feet away from his reach. Rehearse several exchanges for unguarded objects, always keeping the object near you and a couple of feet beyond his reach. Then do the same using the lowest value previously guarded object

            If the dog guards, practice Step 6 from six to ten feet away, increasing distance as much as is needed to get tension free "exchanges." Gradually decrease distance until you are doing successful exchanges from a couple of feet away

Step 7:   Hand object used in Step 6 to dog without letting go. As soon as his mouth touches it, calmly take it back, praise warmly, supply high value treat and immediately repeat

Step 8:   Hand same object to dog, let go for a half second, take object away, cheer dog for his unparalleled genius, supply treat and repeat

Step 9:   Hand same object to dog, let go for 1-2 seconds, then take object away etc.

Step 10:   Hand same object to dog, let go for 5 seconds, then take object away etc.

Step 11:   Hand same object to dog, let go for 10 seconds, then take object away etc.

Step 12:   Hand same object to dog, stand up, withdraw to 6 feet away for 1 second, then approach, bend over, take object away etc.

If guarding spikes on this step, practice trials of standing up, then immediately bending over and taking object away without withdrawing

Step 13:   Hand same object to dog, withdraw to 10 feet for 1 second, then approach etc.

Step 14:   Hand same object to dog, withdraw to 20 feet for 1 second, then approach etc.

Step 15:   Hand same object to dog, withdraw to 6 feet for 5 seconds, then approach etc.

Step 16:   Hand same object to dog, withdraw to 6 feet for 10 seconds, then approach etc.

Step 17:   Hand same object to dog, withdraw to 6 feet for 20 seconds, then approach etc.

Step 18:   Hand same object to dog, withdraw to 6 feet for 30 seconds, then approach etc.

Step 19:   Hand same object to dog, withdraw to 10 feet for 5 seconds, then approach etc.

Step 20:   Hand same object to dog, withdraw to 10 feet for 10 seconds, then approach etc.

Step 21:   Hand same object to dog, withdraw to 10 feet for 20 seconds, then approach etc.

Step 22:   Hand same object to dog, withdraw to 10 feet for 30 seconds, then approach etc.

Step 23:   Hand same object to dog, withdraw to 20 feet for 10 seconds, then approach etc.

Step 24:   Hand same object to dog, withdraw to 20 feet for 20 seconds, then approach etc.

Step 25:   Hand same object to dog, withdraw to 20 feet for 30 seconds, then approach etc.

Step 26:   Hand same object to dog, leave room for 10 seconds, then approach etc.

Step 27:   Hand same object to dog, leave room for 30 seconds, then approach etc.

Step 28:   Plant same object in room and let dog take possession spontaneously. As soon as he does, approach etc.

Step 29:   Plant same object in room and let dog take possession spontaneously. Wait 30 seconds, then approach etc.

Step 30:   Plant same object in room and let dog take

possession spontaneously. Wait 1 – 2 minutes, then approach etc.

Level Two: Beginning with Step 6, complete the above hierarchy for all lowest value guarded objects – you may be able to alternate objects within a session at this stage; however, if this proves problematic, stick to the same object for now (note: if all guarded objects are intensely guarded, simply switch to another one)

Level Three: Beginning with Step 6, complete the above hierarchy for all severely guarded objects

Level Four: Beginning with Step 6, complete the above hierarchy using novel, high value objects

Level Five: Beginning with Step 6, complete the above hierarchy off muzzle for least, moderately, severely guarded and novel objects

At this point you can switch to doing strictly cold trials, where you spot check the dog when he is already dug in with objects, each time supplying a delicious surprise before giving him his object back. If you find you must remove an object that you are not prepared to give back, supply a super-good reward and then replace the forbidden object with a legal one. If you find you must do this when you are not armed with good bait, such as out on the street, don't sweat it too much. Pour on the praise and rehearse a couple of paid off exchanges when you are next able. If, during spot checks, there is ever any small sign of guarding, it should immediately be addressed with remedial exercises. We'll discuss maintenance and regressions in more detail later.

You will find when working on hierarchies that you are often inserting intermediate steps at sticky spots, such as when you first completely let go of an object or when you first approach from a distance after some substantial duration. These are big landmarks. And, when you construct a hierarchy, it is an estimate and will be tailored to the individual dog through intermediate step insertion as you go along. You may also notice acceleration in the overall pace as you go through the exercises, allowing more rapid criteria raises with a more experienced dog.

One feature you might have noticed about the sample hierarchies provided is the way new criteria are added. If one parameter is made significantly more difficult, some other one will be made easier. For instance, when initiating back touches for the first time, the distance from which the trainer approaches is reduced. When switching to a hotter resource, the hierarchy is begun at the very easiest exercise again. You will recognize this way of working if you have done formal shaping by successive approximation.

Location Guarding

The hierarchy presented in this section is really more of a sequence of operant conditioning exercises to fix a dog who guards sofas, beds and other furniture. The classical counterconditioning is a by-product of the reinforcement history you will build up. A dog who guards the car or his crate can also benefit enormously from the placement exercises in this section, as well as from a D&C hierarchy along the lines of the ones presented for food and object guarding. The D&C variables to pay attention to are how

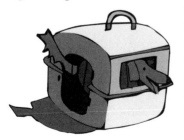

long he's been in the crate or car, the angle, orientation and distance of approach, whether there are also other resources present, how warmed up he is in the session and finally, how close you get to him and whether there is body contact or not.

There may also be a barrier frustration component to crate and car aggression, aside from pure resource guarding, which is also amenable to improvement with these exercises.

Preliminary Target Training

A good way to start placement practice out of the problem context is to teach the dog to touch a target, like your open palm. Once the dog touches reliably, he can be taught to follow the target around in order to touch.

This can be trained much more efficiently if the dog is clicker conditioned. Clicker conditioning is another application of classical conditioning, in this case to develop the clicking sound into a secondary reinforcer that you will then employ in operant conditioning! The two events you are pairing in this case are the sound of the clicker followed by a tasty treat. After sufficient repetition, the clicker can be used to reinforce desired behavior. Always follow up the clicking sound with the treat as this relationship is a classical one, not to be confused with the variable kinds of schedules used in operant conditioning, where behavior does not get rewarded every time (and thus not clicked every time either).

The advantages of using a clicker are well known and include vastly improved timing of reinforcement, the ability to reinforce the dog at a distance and the possibility of conditioning the click to multiple primary reinforcers. For more information on clicker training, read Karen Pryor's outstanding book, *Don't Shoot the Dog!*.

Once he's clicker conditioned, sit with your dog and a pile of treats and offer him your open hand. If he so much as looks at it, click and treat him. Carry on like this, capturing any interest whatsoever in the hand with a click and treat. His interest in the open palm might be minimal at first as his focus will likely be on your treat pile, bait pouch or other hand, which is delivering treats. Don't worry about this. It's

54

okay to occasionally prompt him by waving or "feeding" him your open palm, but this is not necessary for him to solve the problem of what exactly it is he has to do in order to get you to click and treat. Most dogs love this kind of puzzle.

Once the dog readily targets the palm of your hand with his nose, you can rehearse moving him around through space to follow and touch the target. Make him move short distances at first and then travel more and more steps in order to touch your palm and get a click and treat. One, small and tentative step may be your first traveling criterion. Start off playing the palm targeting game in and around the house, while out on walks and in all contexts except around places he has guarded. When he's an ace at this, occasionally ask him to target twice before rewarding him. Then you can begin Step 1 in the hierarchy.

As usual, if the dog's bite inhibition is unknown, desensitize him to a muzzle before moving him on and off locations he has guarded. Once you have successfully completed the hierarchy on muzzle, you may re-initiate it off muzzle.

Sample Placement Practice Training Sequence

Step 1:   Using your open palm target, get the dog onto a piece of furniture that he has never before guarded. If he guards everything, try putting a sofa cushion on the floor and working on getting him on and off that. Gradually move the cushion closer to the sofa until it is back in its customary position

Once he's on, praise only but do not click and treat. Immediately target him back off the furniture and then click and treat. Repeat until he smoothly goes on and off. At some point he may become reluctant to get on, as this has not been reinforced. If this happens, start treating him for getting on occasionally to keep it sufficiently strong

Step 2: Before targeting him on the same piece of furniture, give him a verbal command, such as "up-up," "into your bed" or "on the sofa." It's important that your verbal cue come before rather than during the presentation of your palm target. Once he's on, praise as usual and then cue him off with "off you get" or any other cue you would like to establish. After your cue, present your hand target as usual and then click and treat once he's off

At some point he is likely to start getting on and/or off on your verbal cue, before you've had a chance to present the target. This is exactly what we want. In fact, if he doesn't start doing this after a few sessions, start pausing when you give your verbal cue to see if he'll get on or off in the absence of the target. If he still doesn't, present a faded target, which simply means less apparent in visibility or duration. You can flash the target, hold it closer to your body, higher up, anything that is more stylized in an effort to start weaning him off it

Step 3: Practice on other unguarded furniture until the dog smoothly gets on and off with verbal cues

Step 4: Practice on locations he has previously guarded but at times when he is not settled into those locations. This will mean you must call him over and cue him on first. Place yourself approximately 3 feet from the location

If guarding spikes here, see if you can do the

exercise by "remote control," from a distance sufficiently far that no guarding is elicited. Gradually decrease your distance to the 3-foot mark as he gets more comfortable playing the game in these previously charged locations

Step 5:   When he is slick in training sessions, do cold trials at times when he has spontaneously leapt onto the sofa or just settled into his bed. Cue him off right away and click and treat as usual. Then let him get on to snooze as per his original itinerary

Step 6:   Practice cold trials after he has been dug into the location for 1 minute (insert more modest time increments here if this proves difficult)

Step 7:   Practice cold trials after he has been dug into the location for 5 minutes

Step 8:   Practice cold trials after he has been dug into the location for 15 minutes or more

Step 9:   Cue the dog onto a piece of furniture that he has never guarded. From 3 feet away, reach your hand toward him for a second, then cue him off and click and treat as usual

Step 10:   Cue the dog onto an unguarded location again. From 3 feet away, take one step toward him, reach your hand out, then cue him off and click and treat as usual

Step 11:   Cue the dog onto an unguarded location. From 3 feet away, take two steps toward him, reach your hand out, then cue him off and click and treat as usual

A significant number of location guarders also have body-handling problems. If he does, work on these separately before advancing to step 12.

Step 12:   Cue the dog onto an unguarded location. From 3 feet away, take two steps forward, reach out and touch the dog's back. Click and treat. Cue him off and click and treat again

Step 13:   Cue the dog onto an unguarded location. From 3 feet away, take two steps forward, reach out and touch his head. Click and treat. Cue him off and click and treat again

Step 14:   Cue the dog onto an unguarded location. From 3 feet away, take two steps forward, reach out and pat the dog on his head, shoulders and back. Click and treat. Cue him off and click and treat again

Step 15:   Cue the dog onto previously guarded furniture or his previously guarded bed. From 3 feet away, reach your hand toward him, then cue him off and click and treat

Step 16:   Cue the dog onto the same location as in Step 13. From 3 feet away, take one step toward him, reach your hand out, then cue him off and click and treat

Step 17:   Cue the dog onto the same location. From 3 feet away, take two steps forward, reach your hand out, then cue him off and click and treat

Step 18:   Cue the dog onto the same location. From 3 feet away, take two steps forward, reach out and touch the dog's back. Click and treat. Cue him off and click and treat again

Step 19:   Cue the dog onto the same location. From 3 feet away, take two steps forward, reach out and touch his head. Click and treat. Cue him off and click and treat again

Step 20:   Cue the dog onto the same location. From 3 feet away, take two steps forward, reach out and pat the dog on his head, shoulders and back. Click and treat. Cue him off and click and treat again

Level Two: Repeat Steps 15 to 20 on all previously guarded locations, inserting intermediate steps as needed

Level Three: Practice Steps 15 to 20 at times when the dog has spontaneously gotten onto furniture or into his bed

This hierarchy is for moving the dog on and off furniture. To condition the dog to an owner approaching to sit down on the furniture *with* the dog, gradual steps toward that goal would have to be designed.

Maintenance, once again, consists of cold trial spot checks to "test the system." Touch the dog and cue him off when he is on previously guarded locations, even when you are "sharing" a location with him. Always supply high value treats. If there is any sign of regression, polish him up with remedial exercises.

Generalization

For all these hierarchies, once the primary trainer has successfully achieved the highest level on and off muzzle and/or tether and can do cold trials, she has outlived her usefulness for exercises. Others in the family must be recruited to begin at the beginning. In some cases, the primary trainer will be the owner, coached by a professional counselor, and in some cases it will be the counselor, with the owner – or a designated family member - going second. Each subsequent person will usually have an easier time, though not necessarily without snags. A good analogy is the first handler clearing a path in the forest with a machete and subsequent handlers being able to use that path. Each trip along the path makes it easier and easier to traverse.

It is perfectly okay to have the second (or third) person start on the hierarchy when the first (or second) person is quite advanced, though not completely finished. It's also possible to have two people working the hierarchy at the same level, though in this case, good communication is necessary in case new information emerges or there is a regression. Each person must do all hierarchy elements – neither can cheat by omitting levels just because the other person completed them.

To get generalization, which means that the dog does not guard even if approached cold by a *novel* person while in possession of an advanced hierarchy item, it usually takes at least three or four people, preferably of different ages and sexes, to work exercises, including cold trials. Be advised that if the dog has only had exercises done with, say, adults or with females, he is at greater risk to guard should he be presented with high-level hierarchy scenarios with kids or males. And, as mentioned earlier, all bets are off if the dog is not socialized to strangers or some particular group, and then an individual from that group approaches while the dog has a resource.

Troubleshooting Hierarchy Problems

The most commonly encountered problems in resource guarding exercises are:

- ❏ Pushing the dog super-threshold by advancing too quickly up hierarchy rungs before the CER is well established at the previous level

- ❏ Poor hierarchy design, such as combining multiple criteria, which pushes the dog super-threshold

- ❏ Difficulty finding intermediate steps between a successful and difficult rung on a hierarchy – being "stumped" on a plateau

- ❏ Management failure between sessions

- ❏ Difficulty achieving cold trials

- ❏ Difficulty generalizing among handlers

Pushing the Dog

What I referred to earlier as skating on thin ice in fear and aggression rehab is at virtual epidemic level among dog trainers. Perhaps it's our habituation to an ultra-fast-paced world in general or dog trainers' habituation to the pace of operant installations, or even the relative novelty of addressing these kinds of problems at all, rather than simply managing them or euthanizing the dog. Whatever the reason, beware the tendency to push the pace. You may get away with it for a hierarchy rung or two but the poor foundation will come back to haunt you. If a dog is struggling at a certain step, it is very unwise to advance to the next. It is, in fact, more prudent to back off and do easier exercises and then take a stab at the problematic rung from a different angle, i.e. by juggling other variables. Struggling is defined as absence of the desired CER – the absence of guarding is usually insufficient grounds for advancement to the next step. Shoot for the CER, whatever that looks like for the dog in question.

Criteria Pile-Up

Another common problem is that of working multiple criteria. An example would be working a food guarder who has a nice solid CER to approaches and bowl touches with moderately palatable food and then simultaneously advancing to a longer duration bowl touch with highly palatable food. Not only should both parameters – palatability and duration of bowl touch – not have been elevated simultaneously, one of them could have been bumped down a notch or two when the other was raised. This is good juggling. Sometimes the criteria pile-up is the result of a poor judgment call and sometimes it is just sloppy or non-existent charting of sessions. It is difficult to keep precise track of these variables and so a planned hierarchy and detailed session notes are essential.

Unsystematic training is called "hack" training. The difference between hack training and systematic training is this: when you ask a hack what they're working on they'll answer, "food bowl guarding – but wow, this is a weird and difficult dog – he's good some days and bad others." A systematic trainer will answer, "food bowl guarding with the following criteria: 10-second duration bowl jiggle from a front orientation, with a reduction in the approach distance as the recent duration increase was a big leap for this dog necessitating backing off on the approach distance parameter. Want to see my data from the last two sessions?" The first trainer may not even recognize, let alone factor in and adjust variables such as duration, palatability, approach distance and degree of warm-up. It's all a big mystery blamed on the dog or his moods. If you're not used to charting your training sessions, don't despair. It will feel protracted and cumbersome at first, but will come more naturally with time. You'll find that it will train your mind to analyze behavior and make better judgment calls.

Plateaus

However well one designs a hierarchy, there will more often than not need to be adjustments as you work the dog. It is impossible to anticipate what will constitute big steps in the hierarchy for each individual. If you implemented a general hierarchy on 20 cases with similar presentations, some would fly past landmarks that might totally stump other dogs, who in turn fly past points that were tricky for the former group. You will frequently find a huge discrepancy in the dog's reaction between one step and the next on your basic hierarchy. This is where the insertion of intermediate steps comes in.

Let's say I'm working on a location guarder who has a beautiful CER during out-of-context placement games: he adores being ordered on and off the chair and sofa but is very tense as soon as we do the identical exercise on the bed that was the original presenting problem, even if the exercise is done out of temporal context. Here are possible intermediate rungs to experiment with:

- ❑ Go to a friend's house and practice on a novel bed

- ❑ Practice in and out of the bedroom, gradually edging toward the bed

- ❑ Practice on a chair placed in the bedroom and edge it gradually toward the bed

- ❑ Take the bed covers and pillows and drape them on the sofa the dog has had success on

- ❑ Clicker condition the dog and, from the entrance to

the room, shape the dog to jump on and off the bed

Any combination or all of the above, or other variations you invent, could be done to punch through the plateau.

Here's another example. A dog guards the owner from other dogs at the dog park. The dog has a nice, fledgling CER to the presence of dogs around his owner when the owner is sitting on a bench but gets instant wrinkly face when the owner pats or otherwise interacts with another dog, even if the guarder is not between them.

He could:

- ❑ Practice in locations other than the dog park the basic counterconditioning exercise: a pat for another dog predicts a pat and a treat for the guarder (with any threats gaining an instant time out – if no improvement after a couple of penalties, increase distance between the two dogs so that the owner is further from the guarder)

- ❑ Practice the owner looking at other dogs rather than flat-out interacting with them

- ❑ Recruit someone to help with the basic conditioning exercise at the dog park by keeping the guarder at a distance from the owner – every time the owner interacts with the other dog, the helper treats the guarder (be cautious about the use of high value treats in places like dog parks as it often flushes out any latent dog-dog food guarding in other dogs present)

- ❑ Ascertain whether there is a differential reaction depending on the identity or type of dog and incorporate that variable

❑ Condition the basic exercise at a quiet time in the dog park using a plush dog – then graduate to a passive, familiar dog, still at a quiet time, and on from there

Avoiding Management Failure

Occasional management failure is something we all have to live with. Some really set the program back, and others seem to have a less deleterious effect. Your best lines of defense are to anticipate in advance the likely weak links. Is the owner not fully facing up to the problem? Is the list of items not fully fleshed out? Does the list include items that are difficult to control? Is the owner asleep at the switch on walks? Is there a conflict between some other part of the dog's life and the management imperative, such as a dog with handling problems who must be groomed or have some regular medical procedure done? There are usually creative solutions and compromises. Owner denial can sometimes be reduced with frank discussion, items can be auditioned, environments can be monitored, basket muzzles worn on walks, dogs heavily sedated before going to the vet, and coated dogs can be shaved down to take the pressure off trips to the groomer for a while. This is much more prudent than finding out the hard way that a particular management lapse proved catastrophic in a certain case.

Life is a
Series of
Cold Trials

Cold Trials

We once considered printing up t-shirts at the Academy that would read, "Life is a Series of Cold Trials." We hardly ever get to warm up for the curves everyday life throws us. In martial arts, for example, one might very well drill a defensive maneuver thousands of times and always wonder whether the training will kick in if faced with a sudden threat situation. The point of D&C is to prepare the dog for a real-life situation. It's all rehearsals for the big day. On the big day, there won't be a bait pouch, training location, warm-up or other tip-offs that this is The Game You Are Used To. Our goal is that, on the big day, the dog will act as though it is the game rather than revert to his old guarding response. For this reason, achieving success in cold trials – one-repetition set-ups that as closely as possible simulate a spontaneous encounter the dog might have in real life – is vital.

Sometimes cold trials are achieved as a natural segue from hierarchy work – you simply notice that you can't stump the dog, even on the first trial of the session and even if that first trial is some novel variation. At this point, you start deliberately setting up cold trials to test the system: is he reliable in cold scenarios resembling the initial presenting problem? Even cold and dug in? What about cold and dug in with items that were sluggish on the initial hierarchy, if these proved different from the original presenting problem.

In other cases, cold trials must be systematically introduced, with attendant relaxation of other hierarchy parameters. For instance, if an object guarder cannot be stumped once warmed up in a session but has yet to be successful on the first, cold trial, the nature of the object, distance of approach or other variable can be bumped down in difficulty on the very first trial of each session and then gradually increased session to session.

Generalization Difficulties

The degree of generalization that's appropriate for any given case won't always be the same. For a dog who guards only his food dish, it is perfectly valid to condition him thoroughly for all family members but then adopt a management regime for strangers. This is a much less strong option if the dog has a variety of food items he guards, as the likelihood of a spontaneous encounter with a house-visitor or stranger while out in public is much higher. In this case, it would behoove you to get a more generalized response.

A commonly attempted shortcut is to have the secondary trainers start at some mid-point on the hierarchy or even near the top. You will sometimes get away with this. When you don't, before entertaining other possibilities, including pronouncing the dog abnormal, have everyone go up the full hierarchy. Take careful notes and compare session landmarks with those of the primary trainer. Then, if the dog is generally stickier than for the primary trainer, or sticky at very different spots than with the primary trainer, start digging for alternative explanations. The front-runners are:

❑ Execution differences or errors by secondary handlers

❑ Undiagnosed socialization deficit or discomfort with that individual

❑ Errors in initial run up hierarchy - secondary handlers merely uncovering thin ice that was there all along

It could be argued that subtle differences in execution are part of the fabric of generalization along with the person's physical package (smell, appearance etc.). So, it is only when execution differences are creating roadblocks that it is worth teasing this out as a separate variable. Note that these differences are not necessarily errors. For example, angles of approach, speed of approach, demeanor when approaching and whether the handler is chatting to the dog while working might be extremely salient to certain dogs and cause a regression or plateau at certain points in the hierarchy. They are not errors but valuable grist for the mill, provided they are discovered and broken down.

Inexperienced handlers, a category most owners and family

members will fall under, require supervision early on to ensure they are executing exercises correctly and recognizing the CER (or its absence, a sign of thin ice). This might mean closely watching and coaching initial sessions and booking supplementary sessions at sticky hierarchy points. Handler errors not caught early enough can really derail a program and demoralize clients, for whom nothing is as reinforcing as progress.

It comes as no surprise that dogs are not equally comfortable with all people in the universe. Many breeds, in fact, have been selectively bred to bond strongly to familiar people but be wary and trickier to socialize to strangers. In a society where most serious dog attacks are to people outside the family, one could submit that this breeding emphasis is not responsible, and that breeding for high ease of socialization would be a valuable line of defense.

Sometimes it's an individual that gives the dog a mild case of the willies but more often it's a category of people. Dogs discriminate age, sex, race, dress, gait, facial hair and probably other variables, likely olfactory ones, with ease. When dogs are uncomfortable, it will manifest as anything from mild head-ducking when patted to more obvious shyness to outright spooky displays of growling, lunging and snapping. When someone the dog is uncomfortable around is enlisted to implement D&C exercises, a profound regression in hierarchy progress often ensues.

There are a couple of options, once this has been identified as the problem. One is to embark on a remedial socialization program, essentially performing D&C to the category of people that spooks the dog. Depending on severity, style (flight or fight), bite inhibition, learning rate and how narrow and well defined the category is, the prognosis ranges from moderately good to very guarded. It's also typically a rather slow-moving enterprise compared to D&C for resource guarding. For this reason, consider the other option, management around the problematic category of people. This will largely depend on the dog's day-to-day life and how well defined the category is. Sometimes it's easy to keep dogs from their triggers and sometimes it's difficult.

A combination of the above is my favorite practical option. Lay out and start work on a sound plan for D&C to the problem strangers while working toward generalizing the anti-resource guarding CER to all non-problem categories of people. The latter will very likely be completed and on maintenance while the former is still in progress. The stranger problem will require management as is usual in D&C programs, and this will include avoiding exposure when the dog is in possession of the (formerly) hot resources. If and when the stranger D&C program bears sufficient fruit, have an individual carefully versed in the problem category go up the hierarchy. You may even find it is a helpful adjunct to the stranger D&C program to add the resource guarding game at this stage.

Differences in reactions to family members are also common. Dogs not only guard differently from family members, they respond differently to anti-guarding exercises. How much this is attributable to training ability and how much to other variables is hard to estimate. Luckily, it's absolutely possible for those family members who seem to elicit the worst behavior from the dog pre and/or during treatment to get up the hierarchy. It usually requires more coaching, directly from the counselor. A more successful family member can also help, if this does not create dissention in the family.

Sometimes the generalization issue is a more mundane one: how to recruit people to help work on the dog? If there aren't any other family members in the house, who should do exercises after the primary trainer, if anyone? And, what if there are enough family members but they are not all willing? The answer will depend on the owner's motivation, the severity and pervasiveness of the problem and whether there is an acceptable management alternative. If recruitment proves logistically infeasible, a comprehensive management regime should be implemented.

Let's say a dog X is a very explosive food, object and owner guarder with a fairly soft mouth. The owner has frequent visitors, takes the dog with her a good deal of the time and boards the dog with various friends when away on frequent business trips. These friends in turn have people in and out of their houses a fair amount. The incentive to thoroughly condition and proof this dog is high as the likelihood of resource encounters with a wide variety of people is certain. Another dog, Y, is a moderate and selective object guarder with a good mouth owned by a retired couple who have out of town family in visiting a couple of times a year for a few days at a time. Other than that, the dog is walked on leash, where she encounters the neighborhood kids at a distance, and runs at the dog park.

In the case of dog X, one would hope the owners are motivated to include key friends in the treatment team. The importance of a generalized response must be explained to them in terms of their elevated liability risk. If they have difficulty getting cooperation, the next best thing is for the counselor to do some recruiting, usually of colleagues. Once the dog is fairly slick, then the more recalcitrant friends of the owner might be willing to do a limited number of consolidation exercises with a dog who has already been up the hierarchy a number of times and has a virtually bullet-proof response. In the case of dog Y and limited recruitment options, the way is clear to manage the dog once a nice CER is conditioned with the two owners. The high value objects could be kept away when the family visits or the dog crated or locked in a room to work on bones and rawhides. He could even be boarded those couple of times a year.

Body Handling Desensitization

The principles of D&C for body handling are identical to those for resource guarding. The first task is to divide the body parts and procedures into ones that are already easy, ones that are moderately difficult and very difficult. Recall our list of the usual suspects in body handling:

- ❑ Restraint of body, head, jaws and/or limbs
- ❑ Collar grabbing
- ❑ Head reaches or touches
- ❑ Muzzle and mouth
- ❑ Ears
- ❑ Feet – front, back or both
- ❑ Nail clipping
- ❑ Skin grabbing
- ❑ Hair pulling/grooming
- ❑ General rear quarters
- ❑ Tail

The other variables you can juggle to stay under threshold are similar to those in resource guarding rehab. They include the identity of the handler, the duration of the handling – especially of restraint, how gently or strongly the handling is being done, and the degree of warm-up. Warm-up is particularly important in those cases where you have identified startle as one of the elements, such as dogs who behave aggressively when awakened or when accidentally bumped in the hallway.

It's a good strategy to separate implements, such as a brush or nail clippers, involved in the problem scenario, if any, from the actual handling part. The dog often has an anticipatory anxiety or dread as soon as he sees the tools and doing a separate counterconditioning regimen is worth the effort. For instance, if a dog doesn't like being brushed, he has his original problem about touch, restraint or having his hair pulled, and has developed a negative CER to the brush.

This begs for two separate hierarchies – one to desensitize the dog to touch, restraint and/or hair-pulling and one to create a good association to the brush. Sometimes it's worth investing in new implements to reduce the pre-existing baggage.

If there is a location that is implicated, such as the vet or groomer, once again, it is worth doing a series of trips to this location to set up a new CER before combining this location with even low rungs on the hierarchy. If the problem is severe or long-standing, the location will be a major part of the problem and will take up a major percentage of the treatment time.

 Ian Dunbar puts it well when discussing hierarchies to fix body handling when he says, "If a dog doesn't like having his head restrained, where do we start practicing? Right, on the tip of his tail." Whatever the problem is, to get under threshold for sure success in early exercises with a naïve dog means departing radically from the target procedure or body part. Here's an example.

Head Restraint and Mouth Exam Sample Hierarchy

Head restraint for ear and mouth examinations is a bug for a lot of dogs. The goal of this hierarchy is for the dog to sit quietly while someone holds his head still, lifts up his flews, checks his teeth, then opens his mouth, depresses his tongue and looks down his throat. A tall order.

The hierarchy assumes that the dog tolerates routine touching on other parts of his body. Recommendations for dogs who do not tolerate touch anywhere on their bodies will follow the hierarchy description. Remember to remain on the step you're on until the dog is thoroughly comfortable and demonstrating his good CER in anticipation of the goodie you're about to provide. If it's a small dog, you must add the component of an exam table, first getting the dog used to being on one and then incorporating it as one of your "locations." For medium or large dogs, start right at Step 1.

Step 1:　　　Place hand on dog's rear for 1 second. Deliver treat to dog with opposite hand, pause, then repeat. Always incorporate pauses and long dead periods to rule out yourself and your smelly bait bag as the best predictors of the goodies coming. Practice in a variety of locations

Step 2:　　　Place hand on dog's rear for 5 seconds. Deliver treat to dog with opposite hand etc.

Step 3:　　　Place hand on dog's rear for 10 seconds. Deliver treat to dog with opposite hand etc.

Step 4:　　　Place hand on dog's rear for 30 seconds. Deliver treat to dog with opposite hand etc.

Step 5:　　　Place hand on dog's back for 5 seconds. Deliver treat to dog with opposite hand etc.

Step 6:　　　Place hand on dog's back for 10 seconds. Deliver treat to dog with opposite hand etc.

Step 7:　　　Place hand on dog's back for 30 seconds. Deliver treat to dog with opposite hand etc.

Step 8:　　　Place hand on dog's withers for 5 seconds. Deliver treat to dog with opposite hand etc.

Step 9:　　　Place hand on dog's withers for 10 seconds. Deliver treat to dog with opposite hand etc.

Step 10:　　　Place hand on dog's withers for 30 seconds.

Deliver treat to dog with opposite hand etc.

Step 11: Place both hands on dog's back for 1 second. Remove hands and deliver treat from pouch. Repeat, incorporating pauses etc.

Step 12: Place both hands on dog's back for 5 seconds. Remove hands and deliver etc.

Step 13: Place both hands on dog's back for 10 seconds. Remove hands and deliver etc.

Step 14: Place both hands on dog's back for 30 seconds. Remove hands and deliver etc.

Step 15: Place one hand on dog's back and one on withers for 1 second. Remove hands and deliver treat etc.

Step 16: Place one hand on dog's back and one on withers for 5 seconds. Remove hands etc.

Step 17: Place one hand on dog's back and one on withers for 10 seconds. Remove hands etc.

Step 18: Place one hand on dog's back and one on withers for 30 seconds. Remove hands etc.

Step 19: Place one hand on dog's withers and one hand on back of dog's neck for 1 second. Remove hands etc.

Step 20: Place one hand on dog's withers and one hand on back of dog's neck for 5 seconds. Remove hands etc.

Step 21: Place one hand on dog's withers and one hand on back of dog's neck for 10 seconds. Remove hands etc.

Step 22:   Place one hand on dog's withers and one hand on back of dog's neck for 30 seconds. Remove hands etc.

Step 23:   Place both hands on back of dog's neck for 1 second. Remove hands etc.

Step 24:   Place both hands on back of dog's neck for 5 seconds. Remove hands etc.

Step 25:   Place both hands on back of dog's neck for 10 seconds. Remove hands etc.

Step 26:   Place both hands on back of dog's neck for 30 seconds. Remove hands etc.

Step 27:   Place one hand on dog's head for 1 second. Deliver treat with opposite hand and repeat, incorporating pauses etc.

Step 28:   Place hand on dog's head for 5 seconds. Deliver treat with opposite hand etc.

Step 29:   Place hand on dog's head for 10 seconds. Deliver treat with opposite hand etc.

Step 30:   Place hand on dog's head for 30 seconds. Deliver treat with opposite hand etc.

Step 31:   Place one hand on dog's head and one on back of dog's neck for 1 second. Remove hands, deliver treat etc.

Step 32:   Place one hand on dog's head and one on back of dog's neck for 5 seconds. Remove hands, deliver treat etc.

Step 33:   Place one hand on dog's head and one on

back of dog's neck for 10 seconds. Remove hands, deliver treat etc.

Step 34: Place one hand on dog's head and one on back of dog's neck for 30 seconds. Remove hands, deliver treat etc.

Step 35: Place one hand under dog's chin for 1 second. Deliver treat with opposite hand etc.

Step 36: Place one hand under dog's chin for 5 seconds. Deliver treat with opposite hand etc.

Step 37: Place one hand under dog's chin for 10 seconds. Deliver treat with opposite hand etc.

Step 38: Place one hand under dog's chin for 30 seconds. Deliver treat with opposite hand etc.

Step 39: Place one hand under dog's chin and other hand on top of dog's head for 1 second. Remove hands, deliver treat etc.

Step 40: Place one hand under dog's chin and other hand on top of dog's head for 5 seconds. Remove hands, deliver treat etc.

Step 41: Place one hand under dog's chin and other hand on top of dog's head for 10 seconds. Remove hands, deliver treat etc.

Step 42: Place one hand under dog's chin and other hand on top of dog's head for 30 seconds. Remove hands, deliver treat etc.

Step 43: Place one hand on top of dog's muzzle for one second. Deliver treat with opposite hand, pause, repeat etc.

Step 44:   Place hand on top of dog's muzzle for 5 seconds. Deliver treat with opposite hand, pause, repeat etc.

Step 45:   Place hand on top of dog's muzzle for 10 seconds. Deliver treat with opposite hand etc.

Step 46:   Place hand on top of dog's muzzle for 30 seconds. Deliver treat with opposite hand etc.

Step 47:   Place one hand under dog's chin and other hand on top of dog's muzzle for 1 second. Remove hands, deliver treat etc.

Step 48:   Place one hand under dog's chin and other hand on top of dog's muzzle for 5 seconds. Remove hands, deliver treat etc.

Step 49:   Place one hand under dog's chin and other hand on top of dog's muzzle for 10 seconds. Remove hands, deliver treat etc.

Step 50:   Place one hand under dog's chin and other hand on top of dog's muzzle for 30 seconds. Remove hands, deliver treat etc.

Step 51:   Place one hand under dog's chin and gently lift dog's lip on one side with other hand for 1 second. Remove hands, deliver treat and repeat, alternating sides

Step 52:   Place one hand under dog's chin and gently lift dog's lip with other hand for 5 seconds. Remove hands, deliver treat and repeat, alternating sides

Step 53:   Place one hand under dog's chin and gently lift dog's lip with other hand for 10 seconds.

Remove hands etc.

Step 54:   Place one hand under dog's chin and gently lift dog's lip with other hand for 30 seconds. Remove hands etc.

Step 55:   Place one hand under dog's chin and use other hand to gently open mouth just a crack for 1 second. Remove hands, deliver treat, pause and repeat

Step 56:   Place one hand under dog's chin and use other hand to gently open mouth for 5 seconds. Remove hands, deliver treat etc.
(ease up in one second increments if you encounter stickiness here)

Step 57:   Place one hand under dog's chin and use other hand to gently open mouth for 10 seconds. Remove hands, deliver treat etc.

Step 58:   Place one hand on top of dog's muzzle. Gently open mouth with other hand, inserting finger onto tongue for 1 second. Remove hands, deliver treat etc.

Step 59:   Place one hand on top of dog's muzzle. Gently open mouth with other hand, inserting finger onto tongue for 5 seconds. Remove hands, deliver treat etc.

Step 60:   Place one hand on top of dog's muzzle. Gently open mouth with other hand, inserting finger onto tongue for 10 seconds. Remove hands, deliver treat etc.

Level Two: Repeat Steps 1 – 60 with increased pressure

Level Three: Practice Steps 1 – 60 with pressure and restraint. Rather than simply placing hands, wherever possible, grasp body part as though holding dog still. Depress tongue rather than touching

The likely sticky areas are muzzle touching, restraint with duration and mouth opening.

If you have a dog that doesn't like being touched at all, the initial hierarchy rungs will consist of reaching your hand toward the least worrisome body parts but without touching. Once the dog has a happy CER about hands extending toward him, commence light, quick, matter of fact touches and escalate very gradually. The hierarchy rungs should be finer than in the head restraint sample, especially at the beginning of the program. The wisest investment you can make in any D&C procedure is a policy of very conservative escalation at the beginning of the hierarchy. Owners who are itchy to get to "the problem" part can be a liability if they skim over the early rungs.

Operant Variations

We've already seen one operant variation in the placement exercises for location guarders. Operant conditioning can also be used for other kinds of resource guarders and for dogs with body handling problems. Some of the principles are the same, most notably the parallel between shaping rungs and D&C hierarchy rungs being sufficiently fine to allow for success every step of the way.

The difference is that rather than doing a version of the problem procedure that the dog can tolerate to develop a competing CER, a *behavior* is chosen that is mutually exclusive to guarding and the dog is reinforced for that behavior. As the response develops, the exercise is practiced in contexts that are more and more like the original guarding scenario.

For example, rather than arranging a D&C hierarchy for a bone guarder where an association is developed between approach, touch, bone removal and a treat, in an operant procedure a dog could be shaped to lift his head away from the bone on the handler's approach. A food guarder could be similarly conditioned to lift his head out of the bowl, to back away from the bowl or to sit on the handler's approach. The handler's approach in this case functions as a discriminative stimulus for the chosen behavior, rather than a conditioned stimulus in CER development.

Now, as it happens, a CER will develop to approach as a side effect of the reinforcer used to shape the head lift. This is an example of the Pavlovian collateral effects of operant conditioning. This effect is evident when you observe dogs who have been trained. If the motivator used in training has been positive reinforcement, the dog will tend to have a "yippee" type CER to the training context and cues. If the principal motivator has been aversives, the dog will tend to have an anxious, depressed or obsequious type CER to the training context and cues. It is because of this effect that positive reinforcement and negative punishment, neither of which employ aversives, are recommended to treat resource guarders, whereas positive punishment and negative reinforcement are contra-indicated.

How much the outcome in a resource case treated primarily operantly is due to these collateral effects – i.e. the development of a new CER in the originally charged context – and how much to the shaping of the incompatible operant is hard to say. It is also interesting to note that when doing straight D&C with resource guarders, dogs will often do things like remove their heads from the resource or back

80

away from it in anticipation of the bonus they are about to receive, even though there has been no deliberate attempt to shape for this. This freebie operant could be explained either as an example of autoshaping – which simply means that the approach-bonus association underlies an anticipatory orientation toward the source of the bonus - or of superstitious learning – which would explain the head lift as having been reinforced and maintained by chance: he happened to lift his head just before the delivery of the bonus enough times that he behaves as though there were a head-lift-bonus contingency.

There are potential advantages to rehabilitating resource guarders using operant conditioning. The danger of going over the dog's threshold may be reduced, as the trainer is using the presence or absence of a clear operant, such as a head lift or a sit, as gauge, rather than the presence or absence of a CER, which in some cases can be rather subtle. Another advantage is the "behavioral pacifier" effect – by giving the dog a task to do, it alters the context, lending a fresh start to what used to be about paranoia and defensiveness. Now it's about clicker training. Shaping with a clicker is a high reinforcement, low pressure endeavor, so the procedure itself will have an advantageous CER already established if the dog has done clicker training in other contexts.

There is also the opportunity to use the operant technique of negative punishment on advanced dogs. Negative punishment is the termination of reinforcement or the training session that is the dog's ticket to gaining reinforcement. Where it can come into play is on a case where there already is a strong CER, established either through direct D&C exercises or with an operant strategy. A guarding reaction in a session can be negatively punished by first marking the punished behavior, for example with "Too bad!!" and then immediately grabbing the bait source and exiting the scene. The gamble is that the dog will find the end of the fabulous and steady flow of treats worse than the fact that his threat behavior drove away the approacher. You'll have your answer in the next couple of trials. After a couple of minutes of time out, recommence and see if he is better, the same or worse. This technique will only work if there is already a strong anticipation of a high likelihood of high value treats in this context – otherwise, your disappearance is not bad news. The only way to obtain anticipation of high reinforcer density is a strong history of it already under your belt. This is why the technique is best reserved for dogs advanced in their hierarchies.

Just as in D&C, variables can be juggled to obtain reinforceable responses. In the example earlier on, a dog is shaped to lift his head away from a previously guarded bone on the handler's approach. It would more likely be the case that the dog would be shaped to lift his head away from a less loaded object and then, when the response is stronger, from the bone. Or, the dog could be shaped to lift his head away with the trainer remaining at a distance and then an approach component added. What's important is to select a reinforcement criterion that the dog can achieve relatively easily in each training session.

Retrieving Guarded Objects

An elegant application of reinforcing an operant that is mutually exclusive to resource guarding is the shaping of retrieval in object guarders. If you're not good at shaping, retrieving is an excellent behavior to develop your skills on. Before wading in, do yourself a favor and read *Don't Shoot the Dog!* by Karen Pryor. Here is an outline of how to proceed:

❑ Shape targeting of a specific ball or toy

❑ When targeting is strong, look for nose prods or nibbles

82

- When nudging or nibbling strong, look for mouth contact or better mouth contact

- Shape pick-ups

- Shape longer duration pick-ups

- Shape pick-up and carries

- Shape carries toward you

- Shape traveling to object, picking up and carrying toward you – teach the dog that the object is "money" he can use to buy clicks and treats

- Give verbal cue prior to letting dog see object

- When behavior is strong, teach dog that behavior only works when cue is given (i.e. extinguish off-cue)

- Practice with new objects – go back as many steps as needed to rebuild solid response

- Practice with previously guarded objects – if possible, going up a hierarchy of difficulty

This last step is where the most interesting work starts. When the dog reliably retrieves a variety of objects on cue, give him an item from the lowest level of previously guarded objects. As soon as he sees you put it down, cue the retrieve. Regardless of whether he does anything remotely resembling his retrieve, click, treat and praise as though he were a genius. If he did not retrieve but comes to collect his treat after you click, cue the retrieve again once he's collected his treat. Whatever you do, don't make any moves toward the object. Maintain an upbeat, normal, clicker-training mode demeanor. Set as low a standard as it takes to be clicking and treating the dog every five or six seconds. Try to shape for tiny improvements, which might be looking at you occasionally if he has claimed the resource, putting it down if he carries it off or even shaping his original targeting response if he ignores the object. The important thing is that your first shaping session or two with a loaded object is bursting with reinforcements. The actual standard you achieve is immaterial. It is critically important that the previously charged context of dog plus person plus resource now predict low-pressure and high-reinforcement clicker training with happy handler rather than a tense or confrontation laden scene. Subsequent sessions will look much better.

If he happens to retrieve the object, do a normal retrieve session with it. If you notice any hint of tension or guarding while he is retrieving, such as a reluctance to relinquish once he gets to you, back up and do easier shaping exercises with that object.

In both cases, progress to a different object only when he is as relaxed and reliable with the first loaded object as he was for the unguarded items. This is very much a game of trade-off between the object and what you're offering as bonus so crack out the highest value bait once you commence retrieve work on previously guarded objects.

If there is no progress once you commence on loaded objects, you can try starting with a few sessions of D&C and then, once you are around Step 12 in the object hierarchy (first approach to a loaded object), try a couple of retrieve sessions (having already shaped a retrieve on unguarded objects). If you are still getting nowhere, you can scrap the retrieve training for this case or else try reviving it at a much, much later point in D&C. Another option is to consult with a trainer with some specialization in shaping by successive approximation techniques.

Note that some dogs are natural retrievers. They find playing fetch intrinsically reinforcing. This is not the same thing as the shaped retrieve described earlier. The shaped retrieve is more fruitful as a countermeasure for object guarding so even if the dog has a natural retrieve, shape one from scratch anyway.

Adjunct Measures

There are a number of indirect measures that may be beneficial. In the vast majority of cases, no combination of these would be a substitute for direct desensitization and counterconditioning or properly executed operant techniques. However, all are non-harmful, possibly beneficial from the rehabilitation standpoint and definitely beneficial from the quality of life standpoint.

First and foremost, ensure that the dog has adequate physical and mental stimulation on a daily basis. There is now evidence that aerobic exercise raises serotonin levels, which is good for the cause. Good choices are jogging, dog play, sustained games of fetch, long hikes, swimming and organized sports like Agility and Flyball. Before commencing an exercise program, get your dog thoroughly vet checked, especially if he has been a couch potato. Physical exercise is part of the battle. The other part is tiring the dog out mentally. Most pet dogs get far too little problem-solving and mental stimulation. Easy interventions that can enrich the dog's day to day environment include:

- ❏ Dog-dog interaction. Social problems – i.e. navigating interactions with other beings – are among the most complex and may even be a primary reason for big complex brains in the first place. Dog-dog play is also good physical exercise and keeps dogs' social skills from getting rusty. If a dog has a fear or aggression problem with other dogs, this should first be addressed by a competent professional.

- Games that involve predatory behaviors, such as fetch, tug and hide and seek. These are also good physical energy burners.

- Walks, especially where the dog can explore interesting and novel smells.

- Training – it can be obedience, tricks, free-shaping practice or anything that involves the dog working for reinforcement. Free-shaping is especially fruitful from a problem-solving standpoint. For information on free-shaping, consult *Don't Shoot the Dog!*

- Nothing For Free interventions. This is recognizing that there are other reinforcers in the dog's day-to-day life besides the praise, food and play we might dispense in training sessions. We open doors for dogs, take them places in the car, let them out of the car when we get there, unfasten leashes on hiking trails, let them smell particularly fascinating bushes or clumps of grass, put food and water bowls down, hand them chew toys and massage them endlessly.

  We can initiate these activities without consideration of what behavior the dog is doing at the moment of initiation – and thus what behavior is being reinforced – or we can exploit these opportunities by asking the dog to respond to a cue before initiating them.

Impulse control exercises are often helpful for many of these dogs. Perfecting nicely generalized versions of stay, off or leave it, wait at doorways and tricks that involve the dog having to control an impulse (such as catching cookies placed on his nose), taught using positive reinforcement, are valuable.

Check for and suspend any use of aversives, including hidden aversives, in the dog's life. The concept of "hidden aversives" speaks to the relativity of stimuli. A dog with a high pain threshold may not find a harsh leash jerk to be aversive, whereas a dog with a lower pain threshold may find simply being tugged on a flat collar to be aversive. Even more commonly, a dog who is emotionally sensitive (i.e. a "soft" temperament), may find raised voices or impatient handling to be aversive.

A classic example of a hidden aversive is the wrong choice of No Reward Markers (NRM) in obedience training. It is supposed to be a conditioned negative punisher, i.e. a signal to the dog that the behavior he just did lost him a reward. It is paired with reward removal the same way that a clicker is paired with reward presentation, hence the term *conditioned* negative punisher. A frequently used NRM is a quick "AH! AH!" sound. Although the intention is for the sound to acquire punishing properties through pairing with the primary punisher of reward termination or removal, for a soft dog, the sound itself may be a primary positive punisher. In such cases, it is advisable to use a more neutral NRM, such as "too bad!" or "try again" to avoid the aversive.

In the most severe, refractory guarding cases, consider the use of psychotropic medications to facilitate the D&C program. Once the problem is resolved, the dog is gradually tapered off the drug. Contact the American College of Veterinary Behaviorists if your veterinarian is not experienced or comfortable with the use of psychotropic medications. They can advise your vet or refer you to a certified veterinary behaviorist.

Maintenance and Regressions

Most resource guarding can be resolved using the techniques described in this manual. Once the exercises are completed, the dog will present as a non-guarder, appearing as though he never had the problem. The new CER or competing operant response might be the only tip off that the dog ever guarded. This rosy state of affairs will not last in most cases, however, if maintenance exercises are not done. The behavior can get rusty. Maintenance consists of occasional one-trial spot checks with a pay-off, to keep the CER alive.

I recommend a maintenance regimen of "testing the system" once a week with a cold trial exchange or addition. Some owners do cold trials less often and get away with it but weekly checking is preferable. It's easy to incorporate cold trials into the dog's regular routine. For example, at mealtimes, someone in the family can approach the dog while he is eating and dump a small bonus into his dish. Likewise, dogs can be ordered off furniture and beds for surprise treats and have coveted objects exchanged for a bit of leftovers.

On the maintenance cold trial, if the desired CER is evident and there is no guarding, all is well. If you notice any tension or guarding, however slight, treat it as a bone fide regression. Luckily, tidying up a regression is imminently faster than rehabbing the guarding from scratch. The most diligent course of action is to go back up the hierarchy, starting at a point where the dog demonstrates no guarding. But, unlike initial training, one or two repetitions at each step is often sufficient. What might have taken weeks and weeks the first time is now done in one brief session. Once the dog is successfully at the level where the problem occurred, commence daily cold trial spot checks for a week to ensure the refresher has stuck. Dogs who demonstrate that they are prone to regressions should be maintained with more frequent cold trials. I suggest once a day.

Another kind of post-treatment regression involves the guarding flaring up for a novel person. Sometimes this will be a tip-off that the dog is not full socialized and therefore finds the proximity of a certain person inherently threatening. Careful history will usually reveal whether this is the case. If it is, the options are to manage that category of people around the dog when resources are involved or treat the underlying socialization omission. In some cases, the dog's discomfort is sufficiently severe that prudence dictates treating the problem.

If there is no underlying fear or dislike of the particular person (implying their category), then the best solution is to recruit that person, if he is willing, to do a few exercises. People often find the recruiting aspect extremely awkward, but I would urge trainers to exploit this valuable opportunity for consolidating training whenever possible. It is much less desirable to manage in this instance, although this is the fall-back position if recruiting is not possible.

Body Handling Prevention Exercises

Most adult resource guarders and dogs with body handling issues, including the most severe, presented normally as puppies. It is therefore prudent to institute large-scale prevention. *All* puppies should be systematically handled, groomed, body restrained, head restrained, examined, poked and prodded by a wide variety of people, especially children. Every attempt should be made to create a positive CER by pairing the ministrations with tasty treats, play and praise. It is very much like doing D&C at an ultra fast pace. Should the puppy be fearful or reluctant about any particular procedure or body part, extra attention is a must. Don't brush these flags under the rug, hoping that the puppy will spontaneously improve with age. There is no higher priority for a puppy presenting with body handling discomfort than full-scale intervention.

There is no excuse for any dog to have a bad first impression of the veterinarian's, groomer's, baths or small kids' hands. First impressions are extremely potent. Arrange the firsts to be good ones, which may mean scheduling trips to the veterinarian and groomer just to hang out, meet people, be patted and get treats. By the time the puppy goes in for examination and vaccinations, he will have been prepped for the handling part with exercises and for the location with the fun excursion(s).

Guarding Prevention

Here are standard anti-resource guarding measures for use with puppies and all non-guarding adults:

- ❏ Chew toy and bone exchanges: identical to spot checks for reformed guarders, regular one-trial exchanges for tasty treats are the first line of defense against object guarding. All family members should participate.

- ❏ Food bowl bonuses: While the dog is eating, approach and add a bonus consisting of something more palatable than what is in his bowl. The addition can be just dumped in or the bowl can be removed, the bonus added and the bowl returned to the dog. The ideal is to alternate. Again, all family members should participate.

- ❏ Chew-toy and bone sharing: sit on the floor and hold a rawhide for the dog while he chews it. Many dogs like the added convenience. Even better, handle the dog with your free hand while he chews.

- ❏ Situational awareness: when out on walks, try to scope for hideous gutter garbage like fast food wrappers and remains so you are never forced to extract from the dog really fascinating stuff that you cannot give back.

- ❏ Bite inhibition conditioning for puppies: teach

puppies to play bite softly before teaching them not to play bite at all. For more information, see the works of Dr. Ian Dunbar and get your puppy into a reputable puppy class.

Resources

If you have a dog with a resource guarding problem, here is a list of organizations that can help you locate a counselor in your area. Keep in mind that membership in these organizations does not necessarily mean a given individual is competent at applying the principles described in this manual.

The Academy for Dog Trainers
www.academyfordogtrainers.com

Association of Pet Dog Trainers (APDT)
17000 Commerce Parkway, Suite C
Mt. Laurel, NJ 08054
1-800-PET-DOGS
Fax: 856-439-0525
www.apdt.com

Animal Behavior Society (ABS)
812-856-5541
Fax : 812-856-5542
www.animalbehavior.org

American College of Veterinary Behaviorists
979-845-2351
Fax: 979-845-6978
E-mail: bbeaver@cvm.tamu.edu

Supplementary Reading

There is an impressive amount of dead wrong information out there on dog behavior and training. It would appear that in order for an idea or technique to gain a following, it doesn't have to be true; it only has to be catchy. So, it bears remembering when scoping for dog training books that just because it's in print does not mean it has any relationship to known principles of how animals learn or of dog ethology. Here is a sampling of the better books out there:

Abrantes, Roger, *Dog Language*

Borchelt & Voith, *Readings in Companion Animal Behavior*

Dodman, Nicholas, *The Dog Who Loved Too Much*

Dunbar, Ian, *How to Teach a New Dog Old Tricks*

Hetts, Suzanne, *Pet Behavior Protocols*

Miller, Pat, *The Power of Positive Dog Training*

Pryor, Karen, *Don't Shoot the Dog!*

Reid, Pamela, *Excel-Erated Learning*

Serpell, James, *The Domestic Dog*

The best source I know for good dog books and videos is:

Dogwise
1-800-776-2665
www.dogwise.com

The following two hierarchies are adapted from those of Gina Phairas, Rehabilitation Coordinator at The San Francisco SPCA's Behavior and Training Department. The first is a set of suggested shaping rungs for modifying food guarding using operant conditioning. The second, for hand-shyness, was created for an individual dog. This dog had been clicker conditioned and so this was incorporated – the hierarchy would work equally well without a clicker.

Appendix I
Differential Reinforcement of an Operant Incompatible with Food Bowl Guarding

Preliminary Impulse Control Exercises

Install: 1) an automatic sit-stay with presentation of empty bowl as cue, 2) "okay" as stay release, and 3) No-Reward Mark (such as "too bad") to signal no reinforcer when stay is broken

Proof auto sit-stay with handler movement, then with bowl movement

Exercises

1. Add duration to empty bowl presentation, i.e. put bowl down and hold onto it before reinforcing sit
2. Withdraw hand for 1-2 seconds and then re-touch bowl before reinforcing sit
3. Withdraw hand and take one stride back, then re-approach and re-touch bowl before reinforcing sit
4. Dog in possession of bowl at beginning of session rather than handler presenting bowl – reinforce auto-sit on approach (may need to prompt initially)
5. Approach bowl, remove and replace before reinforcing sit

Note: If the dog has no body handling issues, proceed. If handling issues are present, these must be formally addressed before progressing.

6. Body touches with bowl present
7. Approach and touch dog before reinforcing sit
8. Approach and handle dog before reinforcing sit
9. Generalization and other proofing variations as desired
10. Maintenance with reinforced spot checks during meals

Levels to cover:

- Empty bowl, on tie-down, full dog (post-meal)
- Empty bowl, on tie-down, hungry dog
- Dry kibble, on tie-down, full dog
- Dry/wet mix, on tie-down, full dog
- Empty bowl, on tie-down, hungry dog
- Dry kibble, on tie-down, hungry dog
- Dry/wet mix, on tie-down, hungry dog
- Empty bowl, without tie-down, hungry dog
- Dry kibble, without tie-down, hungry dog
- Dry/wet mix, without tie-down, hungry dog

Note: Don't forget to consistently trump whatever is in the bowl with a significantly higher value reinforcer. Impasses, such as proceeding from empty bowl to kibble-in-bowl or from kibble to more palatable food, can be navigated by:

- Finer incremental increases of wet/dry percentages
- Finer manipulations of degree of satiation

Appendix II
Handling Hierarchy for Severe Hand-Shyness

Work sitting, avoiding any extra movement. Do not continue from one step to another until the dog demonstrates the yippee response consistently at the step you are already on. Remember that each dog's yippee response may differ.

1. Slowly lift right hand, 3 inches from the right side of your body, C/T (click & treat – toss/drop treat)
2. Slowly lift right hand, 3 inches from the left side of your body, C/T
3. Slowly lift right hand, 6 inches from the right side of your body, C/T
4. Slowly lift right hand, 6 inches from the left side of your body, C/T
5. Slowly lift left hand, 3 inches from the right side of your body, C/T
6. Slowly lift left hand, 3 inches from the left side of your body, C/T
7. Slowly lift left hand, 6 inches from the right side of your body, C/T
8. Slowly lift left hand, 6 inches from the left side of your body, C/T
9. Slowly lift your right hand straight up, 3 inches, C/T
10. Slowly lift your right hand straight up, 6 inches, C/T
11. Slowly lift your left hand straight up, 3 inches, C/T
12. Slowly lift your left hand straight up, 6 inches, C/T
13. Slowly lift you left hand above your head, C/T
14. Lift hands from various directions, in random order, C/T after each hand raise
15. Lift hand from various directions gradually increasing the speed of the hand raise
16. *Cold trial hand lifts from all directions*

17. Reach toward the face stopping six inches from side of head (right side then left), C/T
18. Reach toward face stopping three inches from side of

head (right side then left), C/T

19. Reach toward face stopping 2 inches from side of head (right side then left), C/T
20. Reach toward face stopping one inch from side of head (right side then left), C/T
21. Reach toward face, one-second face touch, (right side then left), C/T
22. *Cold trial face touches*

23. Reach toward chin stopping six inches from chin, C/T
24. Reach toward chin stopping one inch from chin, C/T
25. Reach under chin and touch for one second, C/T
26. Reach toward chin and touch for two seconds, C/T
27. *Cold trial chin touches*

28. Reach toward collar stopping 5 inches from collar, C/T (reach from various directions)
29. Reach toward collar stopping 3 inches from collar, C/T (reach from various directions)
30. Reach toward collar stopping 3 inches from collar, C/T (reach from various directions)
31. One-second collar touch, C/T (reach from various directions)
32. Two-second collar touch, C/T (reach from various directions)
33. *Cold trial collar touches*

34. Reach toward collar while holding leash, stop 5 inches from collar, C/T (reach from various directions)
35. Reach toward collar while holding leash, stop 3 inches from collar, C/T (reach from various directions)
36. Reach toward collar while holding leash, stop 3 inches from collar, C/T (reach from various directions)
37. One-second collar touch with leash (do not clip the leash), C/T (reach from various directions)
38. Two-second collar touch with leash (do not clip the leash), C/T (reach from various directions)
39. *Cold trial collar touches with leash*

40. Clip leash on, C/T, immediately remove
41. Clip leash on for one-second, C/T
42. Clip leash on for two-seconds, C/T
43. Clip leash on for three-seconds, C/T
44. Clip leash on for five-seconds, C/T
45. Cold Trial Leash Clipping
46. From seated position, begin to stand, stopping ¼ of the way to your stand, C/T
47. From seated position, begin to stand, stopping ½ of the way to your stand, C/T
48. From seated position, begin to stand, stopping 3/4 of the way to your stand, C/T
49. From the seated position, slowly stand, C/T
50. From the seated position, stand more quickly, C/T
51. *Cold trial standing from seated position*

52. From a stand, lean toward dog, C/T
53. From a stand, move one foot toward dog 6 inches, C/T (from various directions)
54. Move one foot toward dog, C/T (from various directions)
55. Move one full step toward dog, C/T (from various directions)
56. Take two steps toward dog, C/T (from various directions)
57. Take three steps toward dog, C/T (from various directions)
58. Take four steps toward dog, C/T (from various directions)
59. *Cold trial approaches*

60. Approach dog from one foot and reach toward her stopping 12 inches from her face, C/T
61. Approach dog from one foot and reach toward her stopping 6 inches from her face, C/T
62. Approach dog from one foot and reach toward her stopping 3 inches from her face, C/T
63. Approach dog from one foot and reach toward her

stopping 2 inches from her face, C/T
64. Approach dog from one foot and reach toward her stopping 1 inch from her face, C/T
65. Approach dog from one foot and touch her face, C/T
66. *Cold trial face touches with one foot approach*

67. Approach dog from three feet and reach toward her stopping 12 inches from her face, C/T
68. Approach dog from three feet and reach toward her stopping 6 inches from her face, C/T
69. Approach dog from three feet and reach toward her stopping 3 inches from her face, C/T
70. Approach dog from three feet and reach toward her stopping 2 inches from her face, C/T
71. Approach dog from three feet and reach toward her stopping 1 inch from her face, C/T
72. Approach dog from three feet and touch her face, C/T
73. *Cold trial face touches with three foot approach*

74. Approach dog from five feet and reach toward her stopping 12 inches from her face, C/T
75. Approach dog from five feet and reach toward her stopping 6 inches from her face, C/T
76. Approach dog from five feet and reach toward her stopping 3 inches from her face, C/T
77. Approach dog from five feet and reach toward her stopping 2 inches from her face, C/T
78. Approach dog from five feet and reach toward her stopping 1 inch from her face, C/T
79. Approach dog from five feet and touch her face, C/T
80. *Cold trial face touches with five foot approach*

81. Approach dog from one foot and reach toward her stopping 12 inches from her collar, C/T
82. Approach dog from one foot and reach toward her stopping 6 inches from her collar, C/T
83. Approach dog from one foot and reach toward her stopping 3 inches from her collar, C/T

84. Approach dog from one foot and reach toward her stopping 2 inches from her collar, C/T
85. Approach dog from one foot and reach toward her stopping 1 inch from her collar, C/T
86. Approach dog from one foot and touch her collar, C/T
87. *Cold trial collar touches with one foot approach*

88. Approach dog from three feet, reach toward her stopping 12 inches from her collar, C/T
89. Approach dog from three feet and reach toward her stopping 6 inches from her collar, C/T
90. Approach dog from three feet and reach toward her stopping 3 inches from her collar, C/T
91. Approach dog from three feet and reach toward her stopping 2 inches from her collar, C/T
92. Approach dog from three feet and reach toward her stopping 1 inch from her collar, C/T
93. Approach dog from three feet and touch collar, C/T
94. *Cold trial collar touches with three foot approach*

95. Approach dog from five feet and reach toward her stopping 12 inches from her collar, C/T
96. Approach dog from five feet and reach toward her stopping 6 inches from her collar, C/T
97. Approach dog from five feet and reach toward her stopping 3 inches from her collar, C/T
98. Approach dog from five feet and reach toward her stopping 2 inches from her collar, C/T
99. Approach dog from five feet and reach toward her stopping 1inch from her collar, C/T
100. Approach dog from five feet and touch her collar, C/T
101. *Cold trial collar touches with five foot approach*

102. Approach dog from three feet and reach toward her with the leash stopping 12 inches from her collar, C/T

103. Approach dog from three feet and reach toward her with the leash stopping 6 inches from her collar, C/T
104. Approach dog from three feet and reach toward her with the leash stopping 3 inches from her collar, C/T
105. Approach dog from three feet and reach toward her with the leash stopping 2 inches from her collar, C/T
106. Approach dog from three feet and reach toward her with the leash stopping 1 inch from her collar, C/T
107. Approach dog from three feet and touch her collar with the leash, C/T
108. Approach dog from three feet and clip the leash to her collar, C/T
109. *Cold trial leash clip with three foot approach*

110. Approach dog from five feet and reach toward her with the leash stopping 12 inches from her collar, C/T
111. Approach dog, C/T
112. Approach dog from five feet and reach toward her with the leash stopping 3 inches from her collar, C/T
113. Approach dog from five feet and reach toward her with the leash stopping 2 inches from her collar, C/T
114. Approach dog from five feet and reach toward her with the leash stopping 1   inch from her collar, C/T
115. Approach dog from five feet and touch her collar with the leash, C/T
116. Approach dog from five feet and clip the leash to her collar, C/T
117. *Cold trial leash clip with five foot approach*

118. Generalization and maintenance

About the Author

Jean Donaldson has over 30 years experience in dog behavior and training and is the Founder and Director of the San Francisco SPCA Academy for Dog Trainers. Jean's award winning books include *The Culture Clash, Oh Behave!* and *Dogs are From Neptune.* She lives in the San Francisco Bay Area with her Chow, Buffy. Visit www.jeandonaldson.com to keep up to date with Jean and her work.